This Book is Donated By

JUMPSTART YOUR CAREER IN DATA CENTERS

Featuring Careers for Women, Trades, and Vets in Tech and Data Centers

CARRIE GOETZ

Copyright © 2022 Carrie Goetz

ALL RIGHTS RESERVED. This book contains material protected under International and Federal Copyright Laws and Treaties. Any unauthorized reprint or use of this material is prohibited. No part of this book may be reproduced or transmitted in any form or by any means, electronic or mechanical, including photocopying, recording, or by any information storage and retrieval system, without express written permission from the author/publisher.

ISBN: 978-1-64184-847-3 (Hardback)
ISBN: 978-1-64184-848-0 (Paperback)
ISBN: 978-1-64184-849-7 (Ebook)
ISBN: 979-8-9873756-0-0 (Hardcover color edition)
ISBN: 979-8-9873756-1-7 (Paperback color edition)

FOREWORD

This book is a culmination of a career's worth of wisdom, much of it shared by some brilliant minds of kind souls who cared enough to share. This industry is vast and changes often. In fact, it often reinvents itself. Old things become new ones with improvements. There is never a dull moment. (Well, maybe one or two.)

As such, update all standards and double-check vendors for newer technology. Much of the technology mentioned can be implemented in various ways. The reason for the book is simple: there is a massive lack of talent in the industry! There is also a lack of diversity, and despite our best efforts, we are years away from gender parity within technology. While this book contains wisdom for everyone, some special sections address opportunities for underrepresented groups for these reasons. As you notice, there is a shoutout to women, trades, and veterans. All three groups are in high demand to answer diversity and skills needs. But this book applies to and is written for everyone considering joining this awesome industry.

There is a misconception that you have to write code to be in tech. That couldn't be further from the truth. While having some coding folks in IT organizations is necessary, that is only one small piece of the pie. This work is accompanied by three years of podcasts, interviewing some trailblazers. We are also launching "A Day in the Life" videos from folks across the industry. Be sure to check out the videos when they are posted.

7x24Exchange started international Data Center Day to bring awareness of the industry to those who could be future employees. We also have a monitored LinkedIn group, Networking and Careers for Women Trades and Vets (and supporters) in Data Centers. Join us! Find a mentor. Ask a question. Get an answer or twelve. The talent, giving nature, and brains in this industry will amaze you.

Last, I want to thank all of my industry peers who have been so kind as to impart wisdom, tolerate and answer a lot of questions, and for peer-reviewing this work.

Search #DCDayinthelife for videos featuring people in the industry discussing their jobs and what they do in and around data centers.

FOREWORD BY NABEEL MAHMOOD

Computers, whether in large corporations, small businesses, or at home, are connected in a network that has helped us create a global community. Today, we, the people, depend on computing in every aspect of our lives—from communication, entertainment, and financial transactions to education and government services. We are in the data rush era, and this is just the beginning of what the future holds.

As I write this foreword to Carries's captivating book, I share words that I always hoped—and in many ways knew—I would have the chance to write. Already a globally published author, a teacher and frequent blogger, it was only a matter of time before Carrie shared her knowledge of the Mission Critical industry in a book. Her expertise helps the reader navigate the technical jargon, and her passion for the industry jumps out through every word. As she writes in one part of the book, "It's time to move into the guts…". She dives straight into the deep end and gives her readers a front-row seat.

Had such an informative book like this been around when I started in this industry, I would have gone into it a little less green behind the ears. Carrie and I are both veterans of the industry, and I have had the pleasure of working closely with her throughout the years, but she has also become a good friend whose expertise I trust and value. Now the public can catch a glimpse of an otherwise foreign and hidden industry through her expertise. I only hope that this is the first of many volumes.

TABLE OF CONTENTS

Part 1: Background and Terms 1
    What is Mission Critical? 2
    What is a Data Center? 4
    The Data Center Operations Organization 5

Types of Data Centers (DC).................10

Overall Data Center Design Considerations....15
    Codes and Standards 16
    Site Selection...........................17
    Connectivity and Communications 17
    OSP (OutSide Plant) Systems.............19
    Power Considerations 20
    Methodologies for Uptime................21
    Power Sources and Sustainability
        Considerations 22
    Scope 1, 2 and 3 Emissions 23
    Cooling and Water Basics 28

    Physical Security Concerns 29
    DCs for Bees. 31
    Lightning Protection, DAS, etc.. 31

Components of the Ecosystem. 32
    Overall Ecosystem Considerations. 33
    Understanding Power Delivery. 36

Putting It All Together So Far. 44
    Site and Construction 45
    Design and Construction. 46
    Perimeter Security. 47
    The Building Envelope Design
        Considerations 48
    Supporting Building Areas and Miscellany . . . 50
    The Building Systems 56
    IoT aka The Internet of Things 57
    Monitoring via the NOC –
        Network Operations Center 58

Power Particulars. 59
    Sizing Power 60
    Secondary Power and Failover 62
    AC versus DC 64
    Power Monitoring and Stranded Power 65
    DCIM. 66

Cooling aka Heat Rejection. 68
    Types of Cooling 70
    Heat Rejection Methods 72
    On-Floor Cooling Systems Introduction 76

Gray Space and White Space 79
    Fire Suppression 80
    BIM -Building Information Management 82
    Room Lighting 83
    Grounding/Bonding/Earthing 83

White Space / Gray Space Design 86
    Design for Longevity 87
    Downtime 87
    General Whitespace Design Considerations... 89
    Airflow Considerations 90
    On the Floor 92
    Aisle Containment Systems 93
    Raised Floor or Not? 98
    General Rack/Cabinet Considerations 102
    Cabinet Considerations 103

General Information – Active Equipment 106
    Servers 107
    Example of Server Sizing 109

Networking and Cabling Basics 113
    Networking General Information 114
    Storage Networking 117
    Networking and Communications 118
    Ethernet Speeds and Media 121
    Channel Terminology 122
    Transmissions 124
    A Quick Word About Testing and
        Manufacturer Specifications 126
    Shielded versus Unshielded 127
    Copper Systems 129

Overall Cable Plant Considerations 130
Fiber Specifics 130
Pathways and Spaces 134
Cable Routing to Equipment 135
Storage and Storage Area Networks (SAN) . . 136
Data Center Cabling Examples 138
Overall View 140
Wide Area Equipment –
   Entrance Facilities 142

Applications and Operations 144
Cybersecurity 145
Monitoring and Sensors 147
Cloud 148
Data Sovereignty 151
Operations and Management 151
Disaster Recovery and Business Continuity . . 152
Quality Assurance and Root Cause Analysis . . 154
Project Management 156
Coding and Database Management 156
Procurement 158

Resources and Scholarships 162
Trade Associations 163
The Need for Trades, Women, and
   Vets in Tech – Solving the Critical
   Talent Shortage 163
Trades 164
Degrees and Non-degreed Professionals 165
Diversity and Women in Tech 166
Veterans, Spouses, and Their Children 167
Scholarships and Resources 168

    Certification Resources 173
    MOOCs 174
    Podcasts 175
    Talent Shortage Solutions 175
    Mentors and Sponsors 177

Resume Tips 180
    The Interview 182

Alphabetical Job Listings (Some Anyway) 185
    Jobs in Site and Selection 186
    Build (all the above plus…) 187
    Installation and Operations
        (most of the above plus…) 189
    Supporting the Industry 190

Appendix A – Referenced Codes and Standards 191
    Applicable Codes in the US 192
    Applicable National and International
        Standards and Other Requirements 193

PART 1
BACKGROUND AND TERMS

What is Mission Critical?

One definition of mission critical is:

"An activity, device, service, or system whose failure or disruption will cause a failure in business operations."

While other definitions exist, this one, in particular, captures the heart of this fantastic industry. For this book, it's a broad term to describe the data center industry and its supporting industries. The supply of data is mission critical. Access to information is mission critical. The data center industry, aka the mission-critical industry, is the practice of creating, storing, and accessing data via various means. This industry is a well-oiled machine in dire need of workers. As you continue your journey, you will find *mission critical* and *data centers* used synonymously. But data centers are a part of the overall industry.

Anytime you send a tweet, compose a video or email, or save a file to the cloud, that data is stored in a data center. Your photos, memories, evidence, music, along with everyone else's bits and bytes sit in data centers across the globe. But through the years, this industry has remained a bit of an enigma, cloaked in secrecy (ish). There have been strides over recent years to attract more talent to the vast careers within this industry.

This industry is comprised of some of the widest variety of jobs that will never go out of favor or need. Trades are critical in the entire ecosystem, from construction to operations. There are also jobs for those transitioning from the military with or without degrees. In addition, of course, there are ample opportunities for degreed engineers, architects, IT professionals, marketing, and a myriad of other career explanations forthcoming. The point is that if you are looking for a rewarding career, look no further! And if you don't like the job you have, you can look left or right, and there are countless other opportunities within the data center industry. The trick is to figure out what those jobs are and where they exist. This book will help with just that!

A quick glance at job posting sites shows about 350,000 open jobs per job site in this industry based only on the search "data center." These jobs are lucrative and involve every level of education. Diversity is desperately needed, and the industry is working hard to attract talent of all types. Despite being 51 percent of the population, women have not achieved gender parity. The consumers of technology are diverse. Companies that provide technology need the same level of diversity as their user base to ensure that all users have representation when developing products, applications, and user experiences.

Many companies are turning to skills-based hiring. While mandatory for some jobs, degrees are unnecessary for others. People learn in different ways. Companies are dropping their degree requirements, and significant portions of their workforce are either non-degreed or not degreed for their position. Many also offer tuition reimbursement for those employees who wish to obtain one. Trades are **critical** to this entire industry. Veterans, likewise, are also finding their skills and discipline to be in great demand.

Those wishing to work in the industry will find a variety of certifications for various positions and specialties. Certifications are a great way to expand your knowledge. In fact, due to the lack of data center curricula in most colleges, certifications are the primary learning mechanism coupled with on-the-job training.

See the resources section at the end of this book for listings of certifications, scholarships, and apprenticeships.

What is a Data Center?

Quite simply, a data center is a place that houses any company's information. Almost every company has a data center of some sort. A data center can be on premises at the owner's site, leased from a provider, or outsourced completely. Some companies prefer to run their own facilities, while others may opt for hybrid facilities with some on-site resources and others in the cloud. Most are a combination of them. Finally, some entities may decide to operate entirely in the cloud. An oversimplification of the latter is technically running your business with another operator's data center and personnel, but your data. Cloud user companies pay in the utility model: pay as you go. More on clouds later. But for the sake of argument, the cloud is a bunch of data centers owned by a cloud provider.

The data center itself is a collection of electronic equipment (servers, networking, storage, and access) and the supporting infrastructure (power, cooling/heat rejection, building, carrier exchanges, etc.). The former is known as Information Technology, and the latter carries the nomenclature of Facilities. The Facilities department is the department that takes care of the physical infrastructure. That last word, infrastructure, is used and abused and means something different to each department. As you look for a job in mission critical, make sure you understand what infrastructure is under consideration. A networking infrastructure is very different from a power infrastructure with a different set of skills. But in the data center ecosystem, they are intertwined.

The Data Center Operations Organization

A typical *simplified* organizational chart is shown below.

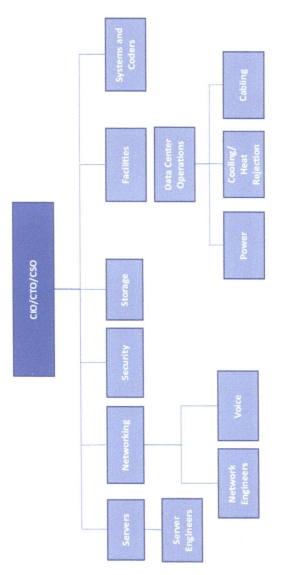

Figure 1. Typical Mission Critical Team Department Layout

The "C" Suite for IT contains the chief information officer, chief technology officer, and chief security officer. In some organizations, these three jobs comprise one position. In some companies, they don't exist; instead, these positions are duties for IT directors and managers—while in other organizations, these services are outsourced to provider companies. We will delve further into each department, but to kick off the discussions, straightforward explanations of the remaining structure follow. Rounding out the C-suite are the CEO and CMO or CRO, although they are not generally considered IT personnel.

Servers Team: This team is responsible for the actual servers and operating systems that house the applications for a company. This team may or may not include security, but all members must adhere to corporate security policies. A company's applications can be inside the data center, cloud-based, or in combination. Often, there is a mixture of server application locations. Server teams are also responsible for the operating systems, virtual environments, licenses, failover configurations, patching, and permissions to the applications used by a company. They are also responsible for evaluating equipment and providing sustainability information to the company. Think of the server team as work enablers or activity directors.

Networking Team: This team is responsible for the flow of information into and out of corporate networks. Duties include selecting, maintaining, and operating all networking equipment, including switches, routers, wide area devices, remote access devices, and communications connections, and stewardship of all addressing for servers, storage, security, desktops, voice, and IoT devices. This department is the transportation, so to speak, of the network. Another way to think of the networking within the data center and across the internet is like the conveyor belts of communications. Routers determine and pass packets (information) from one to another in the most efficient manner possible.

Storage Team: This team is responsible for the company's data. Data is increasingly becoming the currency of companies. Therefore, storage jobs are critical to a company's overall success and growth. Data oversight responsibilities may include desktop data but, at a minimum, consists of all corporate data in any server location. This team will be responsible for the hardware, software, and security of all data and devices, as well as retention strategies and backups. Some storage teams also have database administrators and disaster recovery participants. Think of this team as the town historians, bankers, and record keepers.

Security Team: The cybersecurity team is often an overlay to the entire IT stack. The security team is responsible for all ingress and egress to the network. Cybersecurity should not be confused with physical security, although these two specialties may report through the same structure. Physical security refers to access to the site (data center, building, grounds, mantraps), and cyber relates to digital access to compute resources. As you can see, there will be some overlap, regardless of reporting structures. Think of these folks as law enforcement.

Voice Team: The telecommunications team or unified communications team, sometimes called the voice team, is responsible for communications devices and circuits. If you think of the networking department as the transportation division, think of the voice/telecommunications team as roadworks.

Facilities Team: Facilities and Data Center Operations assure that the environment will support the resources within the site. At a colocation data center, these jobs are handled by colocation employees and contractors. For a private company data center, positions are filled in-house or through contractors. Think of this department as the weather guarantee department. They are responsible for sunny skies and smooth sailing.

Cooling Team: Although these jobs are labeled cooling, in reality, it's all about heat rejection. Compute, network, and storage resources generate heat, and it is the job of this team of individuals to ensure that the cooling/heat rejection equipment maintains the proper operating temperature around the clock. This group controls the room's air balance and handles the equipment's maintenance. The cooling team is part of the capacity planning group along with the power delivery team below. Think of these jobs as your friendly HVAC company. Commercial HVAC technicians are in great demand. Sheet metal workers, duct installers, commercial equipment installers, are all highly desired.

Power Delivery Team: Power personnel ensures that power arrives at the appropriate voltage, remains balanced, redundant (where redundancy exists), and available. This team divvies out the voltage within the space and manages all power delivery equipment. They are also responsible for battery maintenance, failover testing, capacity planning, etc. The power team is also part of the capacity planning group. Think of these employees as your friendly neighborhood electrical road crew. They have similar responsibilities. The power delivery team is often involved in sustainability efforts, equipment evaluation, and long-term planning.

Systems and Coding: The systems and coding teams may or may not exist within a company. But if coding is an in-house function, the team here will be responsible for assuring that all the applications within a company conform to current needs. These coders may work on internal systems and/or the cloud. Many think coding *is* IT and represents the only jobs in IT. We can see that this is far from the truth. This team likely also contains systems designers, database administrators, web developers, enterprise resource planners, customer relationship management, DCIM coders, testing, development operations, security liaisons, etc. Sometimes these positions are outsourced, sometimes in house.

TYPES OF DATA CENTERS (DC)

As stated above, various types of data centers are defined, at least in part, by their purpose. For example, company/entity-owned data centers may be in the main office building, offsite, owned, leased, or even in shipping containers. To discuss types of data centers, we can simplify the descriptions. But keep in mind that lines can blur between definitions and even what a company uses from one month to the next or one site to the next.

Many entities have redundant data centers should the primary facility go down or drop offline. The secondary sites are categorized as hot, warm, and cold. Hot sites are "live" in real-time or milliseconds, requiring simultaneous data writes to each site. Warm sites become live on short notice, but there may be some short delay. Cold sites require a restoration of data to operate. Finally, meshed sites can be any combination of hot, warm, and cold. Meshed DCs are sometimes referred to as fog.

Hyperscalers like Google®, Facebook®, Amazon®, and the like do not build the same kind of data center as a smaller enterprise might build. For these types of companies, their compute resources are their bread and butter and are at a scale unlike any other. As a result, there are some great lessons to be learned from hyperscalers. However, not all that knowledge applies to us average Joes. But if you get a chance to tour one, go! There is simply no better display of the artistry of trades mixed with masterful engineering. Many principles in data center engineering started as an idea with a hyperscaler. The Open Compute Project is a great example.

Colocation or Colo facilities are those companies and entities that lease compute floor space for others' IT equipment. The facilities side (power, cooling, backbone cabling) is the responsibility of the colocation owner, while the IT equipment is the responsibility of the owning entity. It's very similar to renting a house. The furnishings and cleaning are the tenants, but someone else owns the physical building, its power, cooling, and security of the building. These are the landlords of the industry. And just like landlords, they offer different levels of service.

Colo facilities are designed around an assumed power consumption model. Often, an anchor tenant serves as the justification for the build, and then other suites, data halls, and even cabinet rack spaces are up for sale. To occupy the space, tenants may have individual requirements outside of the typical offering for the site. Colo facilities often operate in multiple cities but are interconnected through their own or others' Internet exchanges. As a result, customers can have equipment in various sites communicating with the same provider, as an extension (redundant location) of their own, or redundant to another provider. These exchanges form a wide area network that connects to the public internet in some cases or simply act as a local area network connecting assets from disparate sites together privately.

A provider may singularly own several sites. Some colo data centers are assets managed by a Real Estate Investment Trust (REIT). In some cases, the colo space is literally spare capacity within someone else's data center, helping that company earn revenue from their open floor space.

Provider contracts cover the availability of resources (called service level agreements (SLAs) in contracts), space rent, pass-thru power costs, rental fees, administrative fees, etc. Site fees generally include security personnel. Agreements address additional fees for Internet connections to carriers via the facility's exchange or directly to the carrier. When evaluating contracts from one provider to another, it pays to level the bids and compare features for each space.

Wholesale data centers are those that are purpose-built for others. They technically could be considered colocation. Wholesale facilities are used by large enterprises, entities, or even compute providers. Suppose a company builds a data center later occupied by someone offering services to others (web applications, platform as a service, etc.). This space is considered wholesale space. They are often purpose-built. Some colocation facilities will be retail halls and wholesale within the same building. Admittedly, the lines can be a bit blurry.

Company-owned/Enterprise data centers are company/enterprise owned. The company has decided to own and operate facilities and IT on/within the company-owned property. Often these data centers are within the corporate office building(s). Failover sites for business continuity may or may not be company owned. The enterprise generally employs staff, but duties might be outsourced to contractors. The industry if very cyclical. Some companies that went to the cloud are repatriating their data to their own facilities. Some companies that built out extravagant facilities are moving to the cloud. In five years, they maybe very well go back.

Edge data centers are the new buzzword and are a bit of a combination of the descriptions above. The premise is that these data centers are at the edge, closer to the consumer of each location's data. Streaming services often use edge data centers for caching or moving data closer to those who use it and storing it in faster-to-read memory formats rather than simple disk access. If you look at your streaming service, for instance, you will notice top 10 movies. Those are generally the movies that are already moved to an edge location to increase access speed due to high demand. Using edge services also keeps all consumers from hitting a single site, instead spreading out bandwidth demand across multiple sites.

Cloud data centers serve applications, platforms, and infrastructure in an "as a service" (utility) model. As a result, you will often find the "aaS" terminology for various cloud services and applications. For instance, DRaaS refers to Disaster Recovery as a Service. Cloud providers include hyperscalers and private cloud providers. The cloud is a collection of data centers controlled by cloud providers.

OVERALL DATA CENTER DESIGN CONSIDERATIONS

Codes and Standards

As with any building, some codes and standards help dictate the designs. Codes are regulations required by law. Standards are voluntary, but most provide an open set of goals for temperature, interconnectivity, design, interoperability, lengths, and distances. Codes and standards must be considered in any scenario. Code enforcement is the task of the AHJ (Authority Having Jurisdiction).

If you are unsure about anything code related, the time to work with code enforcement is *before* construction and as often as needed during construction.

Codes would include international building codes, fire codes, electrical codes, etc. Architects and engineers deal with codes and regulations daily. Since this book is designed to be an overview, we will not dive into codes in depth here; just know that they are mandatory. Also, know that regulations vary from country to country and even city to city in some cases. Local codes must adopt national codes at a minimum. Some local codes are significantly more stringent. A design that worked in one location may not be sufficient in another.

International standards development happens through members of the industry and vendor organizations coming together for the common good of the industry. Official standards bodies like ISO and IEEE cover a wide variety of implementations. Trade organizations like the Fibre Channel Industry Association, Ethernet Alliance, Storage Networking Industry Association, and others help shape communications.

As noted, standards are voluntary. Operating outside the parameters of published standards may work, but warranties often site them, and it's an excellent practice to adhere to them whenever possible. Some products are compliant to the standards (they match all parameters) and some are compatible in that they work with the standard but fall outside of performance parameters somewhere. The two terms are not interchangeable and are worth noting.

Site Selection

Site selection is essential. Whether the design is for a company housing their own DC in their corporate building, a colocation provider, or a hyperscaler, there are some commonalities and differences. Ideal sites have access to fiber and power. While both can be added to any location, construction costs are generally the burden of the end user of the services. There are a few exceptions. As we progress throughout the topics remember, you can design for anything! The cost of that design, however, may render some sites useless due to budgetary constraints.

Renewables play a significant part in power conversations in this industry. Overall, the global IT industry consumes an estimated 3 percent of total power. While estimates vary, this is an average and generally accepted number. Cooling consumes roughly 40–50 percent of the total energy for the DC operator. Therefore, selecting sites with low power costs and cooler temperatures aid conservation/sustainability efforts. More on cooling later.

Connectivity and Communications

Fiber is the communication medium between the facility and its consumers. There are many grades of fiber within the data center. Generally, the fiber to the data center will be singlemode fiber capable of transmitting vast amounts of data over long distances. If sites already have fiber in place, then connections are more straightforward. If not, fiber installation will be a budget expense for both primary and any redundant fiber circuits. This fiber runs from the fiber carrier to the facility.

Latency is the time it takes for communications from one site to reach another. While it is important to have communications to the site, the distance the communications are from needed resources may be an issue. For instance, in New York, there is a stock exchange. Transactions there happen in picoseconds and milliseconds. Algorithmic trading is a real time application. Latency can cost millions and distance can render some of these transactions useless. To combat latency, some data centers have limited options for DC locations. Although, in some cases, these limitations lead to more expensive space/land/property. Companies may decide to put only the equipment that serves these latency-sensitive applications in close locations while the remaining business applications reside in less costly facilities farther away.

Fiber can connect to any site, but the distance from the carrier to the site may increase build times and construction costs. Therefore, part of the site selection process should include an exploration of telecommunications capabilities for the Internet, any needed point-to-point connections, and of course, voice and unified communications. Backup fiber can be with an alternate fiber carrier, copper, satellite, cellular, or other means, and of course, latency will help determine the backup communications used, if any.

OSP (OutSide Plant) Systems

Outside plant systems refer to the fiber and communications coming into the building and perhaps connecting multiple buildings within the same campus. Before running any underground fiber, it is essential to coordinate with other trades so that cables do not interfere with existing in-ground services. Pathway planning for growth is also a critical concern. Diagrams and as-built drawings must be maintained for OSP, as it is more difficult to determine paths when systems are buried, especially if there are not metal components that can be detected from above. Rodent controls should be used. Seal conduits to prevent water ingress. Use OSP-rated cabling. It is important to note that, due to jacketing requirements, not all OSP cables can be run past the demarcation points inside the buildings. There may be requirements to convert the OSP cabling to an interior jacket requirement for code purposes.

Running some additional dark fiber/spares or extra room in fiber sleeves is desirable in all cases. Dark strands may or may not be terminated and provide spare capacity. The uplift for a 12-strand fiber cable over a 6-strand fiber is significantly less than paying for two installations.

Some companies choose to utilize blown fiber. These systems blow strands through pre-installed tubes, allowing companies to put in the pathways (tubes) and add fiber as capacity is needed. Specialty equipment is required for these installations.

OSP systems also use specialty equipment to seal out water, make connections, and provide manhole/maintenance hole access. Coordination with building services *prior* to construction and site work is highly recommended.

Fiber installers, duct installers, termination labor, design, and maintenance are all in high demand.

Power Considerations

Similar to communications, power near or accessible by the site will be advantageous and cheaper than creating a new power source. People assume that if power is available, it is unlimited. That simply isn't true. Negotiations with power companies will prove helpful. Some utility providers have monetary and construction incentives for large consumers. Some providers will have additional construction requirements. Power prices include cost per kW/h (kilowatt hour) + transmission fees + demand charges. As energy is said to be ~50 percent of the overall cost of ownership of a data center, it pays to know these costs during site selection.

Some larger-scale data centers build their own substations for grid power. Some may choose a cogen model (co-generation) with the power company. Yet some other DC consumers may choose to generate their own power in island mode.

When renewable energy solutions are desirable, enough land around the building is required. Renewables may be for primary, backup, or partial site power. A current trend as of this writing is to develop microgrids. The DOE defines the microgrid as "a group of interconnected loads and distributed energy resources within clearly defined electrical boundaries that acts as a single controllable entity with respect to the grid." These microgrids can operate autonomously in island mode or provide a backup to the primary power grid. Due to land requirements, renewables are best planned ahead.

With current technology, solar requires 7 acres per MW of power, and wind requires 90 acres for the same MW of power. Renewable solar and wind store power via battery banks included in designs. Wind does not always blow, and the sun doesn't always shine. So batteries store power capacity to supply during non-generating hours. Some types of batteries must be in controlled room environments, and this building/lot space needs addressing during site selection.

Fuel cells are another option using natural gas to convert to power. The byproduct is water. Fuel cells can be primary or backup power. Each unit can be placed in series with other units to form more significant power outputs. Fuel cells are generally leased via power purchasing agreements (PPA) with the fuel cell provider. The provider owns and maintains the equipment.

Generators can be natural gas or diesel. Natural gas is supplied by pipe, while diesel burns dirtier and requires tanks underground. Newer HVO (Hydrotreated Vegetable Oil) shows promise as a direct substitute for diesel. The storage tanks must be cleaned, and old diesel removed or used as the fuel quality degrades over time. Natural gas can be outfitted with carbon capture technologies creating a clean fossil fuel source. Newer hydrogen generators and dual fuel options are coming to the market.

Methodologies for Uptime

Redundancy – Failover in power and cooling facilities is known as redundancy. Redundant components allow a site to remain live if there is a failure of some component. For instance, suppose the main grid power goes out. Redundant power can be supplied by generators. The same holds true for critical cooling infrastructure, also a part of site redundancy.

Resiliency – Failover within the IT stack is referred to as resiliency. The idea is that one switch, server, storage, or other active gear works as a mirror for another. If the first one goes down, the second one picks up the load and processing. Resiliency can occur within a site or from site to site, where one site acts as a backup to others.

Both are critical to any organization. You simply cannot stop downtime via redundancy without resiliency and vice versa. The argument over which is more critical relies on the various configurations, which, at the time of this writing, are nearly factorial, and opinions, which of course, are factorial. There simply is no one-size-fits-all solution or methodology. Needs change. Applications change. Environments change. What was a great idea today may not be the best idea tomorrow.

Power Sources and Sustainability Considerations

The location of the data center will have a bearing on any sustainability goals a company may have. The grid gets power from multiple sources. Wind and solar capacity simply are not sufficient at the time of this writing. Other predominant energy sources include coal, natural gas, hydroelectric, biofuels, and nuclear. In the following table, we see the varying range of power costs.

In addition to kWh costs, consumers pay transmission fees and demand fees. If a consumer generates their own facility power but wishes to use the grid for backup, the demand fee puts that power on hold for their use. Similarly, if an end-user wants the utility to guarantee the availability of a certain amount of power, the power company also charges demand fees. Sometimes these fees are higher than the kWh costs on a bill. Demand charges vary with the time of day, peak hours, off-peak pricing, etc. These charges can get exorbitant when there is exceptionally high demand or the grid is stressed. New AI systems show promise by allowing companies to have the knowledge necessary to orchestrate (move) workloads to sites with lower power costs during expensive power periods. There is an evolving science surrounding workload location and time of processing to save costs and power during peak consumption times.

Scope 1, 2 and 3 Emissions

Being a tenant in a data center serviced by coal makes the tenants Scope 3 carbon emissions higher also based on that coal. Scope 1 emissions are those directly attributable to the company (gas they burn in their fleet, for instance), Scope 2 emissions are indirectly related (charging an electric fleet with coal-generated electricity), and Scope 3 emissions are relative to a company's supply chain. In this case, operating and re-consuming pass-through power generated by coal in someone else's facility (assuming it's a colocation site). Sustainability goals will use these emission scopes in their planning and reporting.

Market	Area	MW Built	MW Under Construction	Avg Power/kWh in Cents	% Renewable	% Natural Gas	% Coal
Atlanta	2,299,692	10	30	4.3	12	49	12
Austin/San Antonio*	1,372,934	121	0	7.3	15	47.4	37
Boston	1,200,000	160	0	15	28	67	NA
Chicago	5,062,500	631.6	18.5	5.8	10	7	30
DFW*	3,784,863	539	0	5	21	47.4	37
Houston*	1,468,207	138	0	6.5	20	47.4	37
Los Angeles	2,500,000	250	0	14.5	33	35	0.12
New Jersey	3,850,000	410	16	7.8	10	75	1.5
New York	1,020,000	152	4	13.2	15	40	0.1
Northern CA	6,375,415	508	181	12.7	36	35	3
Northern VA	31,118,534	2801	339	5.2	4	61	30
Pacific NW	2,579,631	382.7	29.3	7	9	21	20
Phoenix	2,184,076	326.7	32	6.3	14	24	38
Salt Lake City	556,000	80	31	5.6	14	25	61

Figure 2. Top 10 US Data Center Markets with Power Sources

Texas, LA, OK, PA, WV, and OH are the largest natural gas-producing states according to marketed production. Despite tight controls, CA is the second-highest DC carbon producer.

Figures provided by JLL Global Data Center Outlook 2021 and the EIA (Energy Information Administration). Texas state numbers are used as individual cities do not report separately in ERCOT https://www.eia.gov/electricity/monthly/epm_table_grapher.php

The table above shows the top 10 US data center markets. The US has the lion's share of reported data centers. The US also has diverse power sources, making it a good study example. Natural gas and coal are the predominant power sources for these top 10 locations. Renewables are continuously coming online, but not all are grid-connected. The Department of Energy/Energy Information Administration does not list renewable sources in the same way that they list coal and natural gas. Therefore, renewable numbers are from alternative sources, and the overall power source numbers may not equal 100. Minor power sources were omitted for clarity.

Market	Estimated Annual Power Cost	Annual Power $/SQ FT	Annual CO2 Emissions in Pounds for Natural Gas (898)	Annual Spend Coal	Metric Tons of Carbon Natural Gas	Annual CO2 Emissions in Pounds/Coal (2180)	Metric Tons of Carbon Coal
Atlanta	$ 376,680,000	$ 164	78,664,800	$ 45,201,600	35,682	190,968,000	86,623
Chicago	$ 32,090,332,800	$ 6,339	4,968,468,768	$ 9,627,099,840	2,253,683	12,061,538,880	5,471,078
Los Angeles	$ 31,755,000,000	$ 12,702	1,966,620,000	$ 38,106,000	892,053	4,774,200,000	2,165,563
New Jersey	$ 28,014,480,000	$ 7,276	3,225,256,800	$ 420,217,200	1,462,967	7,829,688,000	3,551,523
Northern CA	$ 56,516,016,000	$ 8,865	3,996,171,840	$ 1,695,480,480	1,812,652	9,701,174,400	4,400,424
Northern VA	$ 127,591,152,000	$ 4,100	22,034,010,480	$ 5,103,646,080	9,994,562	53,490,136,800	24,262,967
Houston*	$ 7,857,720,000	$ 5,352	1,085,574,240	$ 2,907,356,400	492,413	2,635,358,400	1,195,391
Austin/San Antonio*	$ 7,737,708,000	$ 5,636	951,844,080	$ 2,862,951,960	431,754	2,310,712,800	1,048,132
DFW*	$ 23,608,200,000	$ 6,238	4,240,032,720	$ 8,735,034,000	1,923,266	10,293,175,200	4,668,954
Pacific NW	$ 23,467,164,000	$ 9,097	3,010,501,896	$ 4,693,432,800	1,365,555	7,308,345,360	3,315,044
Phoenix	$ 18,029,919,600	$ 8,255	2,569,979,016	$ 6,851,369,448	1,165,735	6,238,924,560	2,829,958
Salt Lake City	$ 3,924,480,000	$ 7,058	629,318,400	$ 2,393,932,800	285,457	1,527,744,000	692,980
Boston	$ 21,024,000,000	$ 17,520	1,258,636,800	$ -	570,914	3,055,488,000	1,385,960
New York	$ 17,576,064,000	$ 17,231	1,195,704,960	$ 17,576,064	542,368	2,902,713,600	1,316,662
Total footprint	$ 399,568,916,400	$ 8,274	51,210,784,800.00	$ 45,391,404,672	23,229,060	124,320,168,000	56,391,258

Figure 3. Power Costs and Carbon Emissions

This table shows the same markets but outlines estimated power costs (minus demand fees and transmission costs) and metric tons of carbon emissions attributable to the data centers in the area. A few things are noteworthy. First, notice the differences in power costs per square foot of power. These numbers do not include any transmission or demand fees, which would be additional costs. These figures make it apparent why power costs are such a huge consideration.

Sustainability is a career area with massive demand. We can improve carbon emissions by decreasing demand, improving efficiency, using stranded power, and locating in areas where renewables are generation options. Even with a natural gas supply, carbon capture shows remarkable promise. Carbon Capture and Sequestration (CCS) puts the captured carbon back into the strata from which it came. One could technically create a carbon-inert/carbon-neutral environment with fossil fuels. Carbon capture technologies allow carbon to be trapped and repurposed for use in food, agriculture, building materials, etc. In fact, there are millions in grants for carbon capture right now, with more in the queue.

Decreasing demand comes from consolidating equipment, improved designs, proper server and compute equipment sizing, redundancy only where needed, optimizing environments, automation and artificial intelligence (AI), integrated controls, airflow optimization, decommissioning plans, or any range of measures. Even location makes a difference—the source of power matters.

Cooling and Water Basics

Data center equipment generates heat through operations, just like your laptop gets warm when it it is processing, but on a grander scale. This heat needs to be removed/cooled in some way. There are several means of cooling. But, regarding site selection, some places will be more advantageous simply because they are in cooler climates. Of course, not all data centers can be in cold places and even cold places require some type of air conditioning. With that in mind, sites must allow ample space for cooling equipment and service. When chilled water provides heat rejection, pay particular attention to high drought areas. Always note the cost of water in your decision matrix. Cooling equipment is installed on top of buildings and/or adjacent to the building. Sometimes air conditioners or air handlers (movers) flank the data center space. This equipment is not small.

The equipment's size, weight, and other configuration factors determine its placement. However, the equipment type may or may not be known. Sometimes the site selection process governs the kind of equipment used. If there is doubt about space or cooling capabilities, it is wise to work with an engineering firm, design-build firm, or experienced data center broker before final site selection. For brownfield sites, there may be limitations for existing equipment, upgrade capabilities, fixed limitation of the building structure, rights of way, and other physical restrictions to consider. Brownfield site selection and designs are a specialty.

Physical Security Concerns

The building site should be capable of providing site-level security. These rings of security, as defined in CPTED (crime prevention through environmental design), place the most protected assets behind several "rings" that obstruct or deter access. For data center security purposes, sites should have multiple layers of security, starting with the perimeter. For example, large, purpose-built data centers surround the core building with greenspaces allowing easy observation by security personnel. Data centers within corporate office buildings use the building layers as security stops to accomplish a similar physical security scheme.

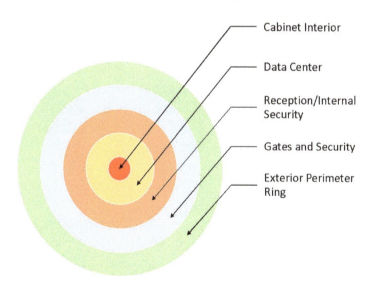

Figure 4. Rings of Security Logical Depiction

For some colocation providers, sites need to be large enough to accommodate growth if expansion is a consideration for the same site. Some will build in other locations and not expand the original site. It is worth having a level of understanding as to the growth plans. Some hyperscalers build in multiple locations to support failover, latency concerns, disaster recovery, and distribute their assets, alleviating single-risk points. Some will build multiple facilities in the same campus.

Risks to the facility location and adjacent property use will factor in decisions. The sensitivity of data may also determine location. Critically sensitive information will have more stringent security rings than other data. While all data is essential, it is not all equal. For instance, Department of Defense data will live in more tightly wrapped security facilities.

Other site considerations include local taxes, support of the local community, staff availability, vendor support, lease length (if leasing), zoning restrictions, distance to public transport, proximity to potential hazards and disasters, etc. Some entities use real estate professionals to secure space. Real estate professionals may have ideas about sites that are not in line with companies' information technology needs. There are specialist brokers for this industry that specialize in finding suitable locations.

Not many years ago, options for data center locations were limited, as high bandwidth connections didn't exist. That is no longer the case. Therefore, the decision to house a data center in a place other than the corporate office building is no longer limited to a few locations (review latency above). However, many companies collocate their primary data center with their offices for preference and convenience. The recent pandemic highlighted the problems of being unable to get to data center locations. While remote services can solve many issues, they may be inadequate. Remote talent capabilities are growing within colocation companies for this reason.

DCs for Bees

Due to the vast amount of land around data centers, one fun sustainability effort is DC for Bees. The efforts started in Ireland. Pollinators are encouraged by the use of pollinator-friendly plants filling the greenspace. The practice is beginning to pick up in the United States as a fun exercise in giving back. In fact, this industry is full of incredibly cool projects like this one. Sustainability careers in this industry are vast.

Lightning Protection, DAS, etc.

Every building needs protection against lightning strikes. DAS (distributed antenna systems) bring cellular inside buildings, which would otherwise disrupt cellular signals. Both are mentioned here simply to highlight additional career opportunities. DAS installers are in demand in this industry as well as professionals for the smart building industry.

COMPONENTS OF THE ECOSYSTEM

Overall Ecosystem Considerations

The data center is an ecosystem of interdependent components and parts. Therefore, while the above descriptions reference the types of data centers, the elements within them are best examined through design and construction. As an ecosystem, there is a delicate balance assuring all components within the environment interoperate successfully. The failure of any single part can wreak havoc on the rest of the ecosystem. Not only do the components need to work together, but every aspect of the data center must also be mindful of sustainable computing and facilities goals. Below, we examine the main components and their relationships to other parts of the ecosystem.

There are direct relationships in operations. These relationships comprise the beginnings of any data center design. Components of design beginnings start with either accurate or assumed IT loads within the space. Even known loads are augmented with assumed load growth. Every server, storage device, network switch, or other active component draws a certain amount of power. The calculations in a purpose-built data center start with known loads. Estimates for data centers built with unknown occupant needs use assumptions for Watts per square foot or overall site power capacity generally expressed in megawatts. As a side note, even if a space is designed to 10kW per cabinet, the loads will vary across the floor, very similar to consumption in a home.

This type of ground-up design is known as a greenfield build, or quite literally from scratch, a green field, so to speak. When a site exists and will be used, even with modification, the site is known as a brownfield. The design considerations for each are different. Throughout the remainder of this text, there will be references to these two terms, as there are some distinct differences in design considerations.

In Cajun cooking, there is a veggie combination known as the holy trinity. In data centers, the trinity is power, cooling, and compute. They are intertwined and the basis for all calculations outside of building floor loads. Since power draw fluctuates with computing cycles, cooling must adapt. These three intertwining components are core for design and ongoing operations and floor balance.

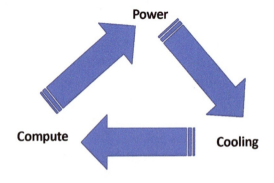

Figure 5. Power, Cooling, and Compute

IT resources (compute) will draw power for operations. As the active electronics (compute resources) consume that power, the operations/chips generate heat. Cooling (heat rejection) will remove the heat from the air; that cooled air then feeds the compute intakes, and so on. Measures of efficiency between the three are often expressed as power usage effectiveness (PUE) developed by The Green Grid. PUE is the total power delivered to the building divided by the IT load.

$$PUE = \frac{Building\ power}{IT\ load}$$

The closer to the number one that equation is, the more efficient the data center operates. These are operational numbers and will vary from minute to minute as compute loads are not stagnant. But averaged over time, the metric helps measure efficiency. Remember:

> *You can't fix what you don't measure. Furthermore, if you don't measure, you don't know if the fix works or how well it works.*

From a design perspective, it is essential to understand that this is the living relationship between components within the space. Designs are based on Watts per square foot, overall MW of power, the land or existing building, preferences, and other criteria. So, to draw a line in the sand, so to speak, if we understand the Watts per square foot or overall power requirements we can get the ball rolling.

Greenfield designs use the overall power calculations to determine floor space requirements. Brownfield designs are trickier; the overall building envelope is predetermined and, at least, relatively fixed. Power assumptions or estimates determine cooling needs. How that cooling/heat rejection happens will be discussed later, but suffice it to say, Watts x 3.41 = BTU/hour. The design also needs to add the power necessary to support the cooling. More on this later.

Once we know power and cooling and compute, the preliminary design begins. As we discuss power, we must determine the primary power *and* redundancy level we desire for this facility. Redundancy is generally discussed in terms of Tiers or redundant components.

Initially developed by the Uptime Institute, the Tier system is a de facto standard discussing redundant components. Tiers 1–4 have equivalent counterparts in other standards (see Figure 6 below). Each standard's redundancy classifications express levels of redundant facilities equipment in order to avoid unscheduled downtime. Redundancy refers to power and cooling assets, failover, and backup components. BICSI, ISO/IEC, and other standard bodies use their own terminologies. The principles of redundancy, however, are the same. Redundancy is rated by components that complete the redundancy equipment with the overall expected outcome being uptime.

Standard				
EN5600	BICSI Classes		Uptime Institute	
Downtime	BICSI Class	BICSI Uptime	UI TIER	UI - Uptime
5 Minutes	F4	99.999%	TIER 4	99.995%
1 Hour	F3	99.99%	TIER 3	99.982%
9 Hours	F2	99.9%	TIER 2	99.741%
90 Hours	F1	99%	TIER 1	99.671%
2-3 Weeks				

Figure 6. Classes of Uptime

Understanding Power Delivery

Primary power to the data center is generally from a power company. It is highly desirable to have the power on a separate meter from the building for monitoring purposes. However, brownfield and in-building data centers may not allow individual metering.

For larger implementations, negotiations with the power company must start early in the selection process. One cannot assume that the power will just be there. The supply is not unlimited. Power needs (or assumptions) and redundancy are vital, as they will factor into power feed requirements and upstream demand. Alternative sources of power generation may apply to a data center build. This power may be the primary site power source, an addition, or a backup generation. Alternatives include fuel cells; natural gas generators; and solar, wind, hydroelectric, biomass, and diesel generators, to name a few. In addition, diesel generators are available that use alternative fuels like HVO (hydrotreated vegetable oil).

Loss of electrical power is a given at some point, hopefully infrequently. Imagine a scenario where power goes out due to no fault of the facility. How does the company operate during that outage? Supplying backup power via an additional power source provides needed uptime. Backup power delivery happens via uninterruptable power supplies (UPS), generators (diesel, bio, and natural gas), stored kinetic energy from a flywheel, batteries, and/or other components.

Primary power equipment provides the main daily power feed. *Backup* or *secondary* are the terms used to address the standby power, and fault-tolerant hardware allows the primary or secondary equipment to come offline for maintenance while still providing the site with dual power feeds. The exact same primary and secondary terminology is used in cooling equipment. The Tier levels mentioned above address the redundancy schemes for power and cooling, with Tier 4 being the most fault-tolerant and significantly more expensive. Most data centers are built with some redundant components. Some are designed on paper to Tier 4 but are not fully populated with fault-tolerant equipment until there is a need/demand for the capital expenditures. Tier 4 facilities exist, but are generally purpose built for a specific need/tenant due to their high capital costs.

Power supplies, plugs, and outlets vary from country to country, as do voltages. If one plans to work for an international organization, pay attention to global codes and laws for power distribution. It goes without saying that the data center won't work without power. From the utility inward, several components work to keep the energy flowing. Some key elements are explained below.

The switchgear is electrical disconnect switches, fuses, circuit breakers, and fault protectors. Power from the main utility supply generally connects to the building through switchgear. In line, one will also find power conditioning equipment that assures that the power supply is at a controlled voltage, removing spikes and dips. Switchgear can kill power to equipment needing maintenance or in the event of a fault. This equipment generally occupies a conditioned space within the service corridor or adjacent to the data haul. In a brownfield or in-building data center, the switchgear may not exist. The complexity of switchgear offerings varies.

Uninterruptable power supplies (UPS) systems provide stored power to systems. UPS systems are between the switchgear and the active equipment. UPS systems will provide power to the active equipment until backup power comes online or until the active equipment can be politely powered down. UPS systems selection is calculated by the amount of power they can deliver for a fixed amount of time. Data center UPS systems work very similarly to a battery UPS you may have at your home. Energy is stored in the batteries. The battery banks deplete this power during outages. Once depleted, the batteries need recharging. If sized correctly, the injected power will keep the IT equipment alive for enough time until the generator kicks in. If not, an outage will occur.

It is important to note that these battery banks are of significant size. Depending on the type of battery used, there may be a need to have an air-conditioned space. Also, a refresh cycle is needed to replace batteries as their rechargeability depletes. Traditional lead-acid batteries have the most prolonged use within the industry. Newer lithium-ion batteries are replacing many of them as the lead can't be recycled. Lithium-ion's charging cycle is shorter; however, the ramifications to Earth are problematic. Newer batteries like sodium-ion and nickel-zinc (NiZn) show promise for data centers and the planet.

Battery bank selection will depend on the amount of power and duration needed. Design considerations include preference, weight, toxicity potential, air conditioning needs, costs, and, of course, power supplied. An alternative to batteries is flywheels. These do not require battery storage and have no cooling requirement, allowing for external installations. In addition, buffer banks can provide the milliseconds of power needed.

Following the power into the data center cabinets, distribution happens via energized busbar, power cables, power strips, power distribution units (PDUs), and the cords to the active equipment. Inside the data center, primary and secondary power are often distributed to IT equipment. However, some distribute primary only, while some have areas that distribute primary or both. More on this later (see whitespace design considerations).

Overhead Energized Busway (aka busbar systems) is an overhead power distribution system utilizing tracks and snap-in breakers for power distribution over cabinets. The track structure that runs along rows in the data center. Outlet boxes are inserted into the track, connecting to the busbar internally to the busbar. The outlets come in a variety of configurations. Cords to the cabinet power distribution connect to these outlets over cabinet locations.

Power panels (on floor shown) are used for power distribution when busbar systems are not. Power cables connect to power distribution units and remote power panels located on the data center floor. Each of these panels contains breakers and monitoring.

Breakers and relays work the same in a data center as they do at your home, although there are new digital breakers that show amazing promise. Because they are digital, they would be able to be accessed remotely, enhancing remote troubleshooting capabilities. Overloading a breaker in the data center will cause a trip/fault. This is why operations professionals must be diligent in power management.

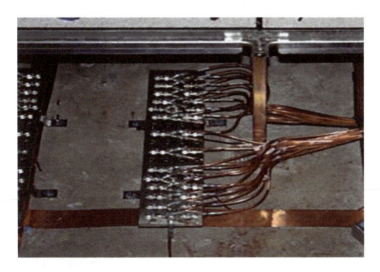

Main grounding busbar and telecommunications grounding busbar (shown) – All data centers, by code, must have a grounding/bonding/earthing system. The terms can be used interchangeably but are country specific. Metal components within the data center connect to the grounding system. Connections include cable trays, cabinets, floor stanchions, shielded components (at one end), equipment chassis as needed, power components, etc. The grounding system provides a path of least resistance out of the building for any transients or coupled current. Busbar attached to the ground gid below a raised floor is shown.

PUTTING IT ALL TOGETHER SO FAR

The above basic definitions help us understand the components, but the real magic happens when we put it all together. So, while we have focused on the site and building so far, it's time to move into the guts, so to speak. After all, the entire purpose of the building is to support the information technology inside. The IT organization roles discussed at the start of this book may seem forgotten so far, but those roles are critical.

In an enterprise data center (company owned) or a colocation space, the IT team has invaluable input. The needs of the organization's compute drive the designs of the architects and engineers. Teams can run current capacity numbers and factor in growth to glean ideas for power needs. When a company selects a colocation space, the processes are similar. A company bases their colocation space selection using the same artifacts of information. Without the basic knowledge of requirements, it's a bit like building a home without knowing how many people will live inside. In this chapter, we will examine site selection and the building infrastructure. Realize that a 1MW data center will have different size needs, but the basics of how it all comes together are similar; only the scale varies.

Site and Construction

Understanding the most basic of needs for power, size, and building requirements helps with site selection. The amount of land needed, utility feeds, availability of communications, and proximity to those services, if they are not readily available at the site, will directly impact construction costs. While some of these calculations will be based on assumptions for some builds, the site selection principles, although simplified here, are roughly equal just are applied at scale.

Although there are some variances between greenfield and brownfield, they both are designed and built using similar methodologies. Admittedly, brownfield installations will have limitations based on the existing building. Understanding the costs for remediation and upgrades will factor into site decisions.

A few other points that may be worth considering are zoning restrictions and the time to change them if needed. Distance to emergency services, mainly fire services, may sway a decision to one location over another. Some providers are choosing locations near colleges that offer data center curricula, as it will be easier to find quality employees. In some parts of the world, the data center is the center of a purpose-built community designed to support the facility and its workers.

As a reminder, you can design to overcome most any obstacle. The cost to do so is the tricky part!

Design and Construction

The facility's design is the work of architects and civil, structural, mechanical, and electrical engineers. There are also design/build firms that will handle the design and construction. Data centers may also wish to consider other environmental factors. Leadership in Environmental Engineering and Design (LEED) addresses the ecology-oriented building design. Factors such as where materials are sourced, types of materials, and reuse capabilities factor into the design. Many architects and engineering firms have LEED-certified associates. This program is under the auspices of the United States Green Building Council. There are equivalents globally including the world green building council, and multiple country and regional based organizations. Additionally, we have seen the emergence of a Net Zero Green Building Council.

Outside the United States, the most common equivalent is the Building Research Establishment Environmental Assessment Method (BREEAM). While LEED certifications use percentages of construction across several categories, BREEAM uses quantitative measures. Inside and outside the data center, sustainability and ecological designs are hot topics with promising careers. The theory of cradle to cradle, where nothing goes to waste, is taking hold. From a sustainability standpoint, there is a myriad of job options within this industry. If this is a passion for you, this industry needs you!

Perimeter Security

For purpose-built data center sites, not only is it essential to consider the environment for construction, but as noted above, security is either enhanced or hindered by the site. Perimeter fencing, automated gates, and security monitoring surround the DC to stop cars, people, and other undesirable activities like protests. The fences act as hardened forcefields. Sensors and surveillance are attached to the perimeter to detect digging, motion, and other adverse security events.

For purposebuilt data centers, security personnel monitor the entire land mass around the DC, as well as those inside the building. All visitors check in via the guard shack, the first line of defense. Visitor parking and contractor parking are also under surveillance. Corporate reception is the first line of defense for data centers that are not purpose-built (standalone). Visitors and vendors should log in and log out for every visit. Entry logs are maintained and retained along with security incidents. Knowing who is in the building is important for security and for any evacuation event.

The Building Envelope Design Considerations

The floor, walls, and roof are considered the building envelope, much like the name implies. It is a physical separation between the conditioned and the non-conditioned space. The building envelope will vary based on the needs of the building, environmental concerns, code and architectural review committee requirements, and preferences. Some cities with large populations of data centers have created stricter guidelines to ensure that the buildings are aesthetically pleasing. Due to the critical nature of the data housed inside, care must be taken to ensure that the structure is sturdy, secure, and supports the needs within the walls.

Depending on the type of data center housed, the building may contain segments known as data halls for single occupants, cages for multiple tenants, or any combination. The building envelope may cover more than the data center for brownfield sites (part of an entire building, for instance) and data centers housed within a corporate office building. However, it is still essential to use good engineering practices for the actual data center portion of the building. In these cases, it is wise to have the data center in an area that requires multiple security checkpoints before entry.

The building should protect the contents inside from the elements outside. Engineering for buildings constructed in areas with certain natural disasters must address these threats. It isn't practical to assume that data centers will only exist in areas devoid of hazards. Construction and architectural principles are available for hurricanes, tornadoes/cyclones, and floods. Although no manner of construction is guaranteed to remain intact, a properly constructed building is the first defense. Highly secure data centers are housed in Sensitive Compartmentalized Information Facilities (SCIFs). SCIF construction is one other type of construction that bears mentioning. These facilities may be all or part of a facility, and these data centers are encased in faraday cages that block eavesdropping and signal jamming. Government and classified facilities are specialized.

Edge data centers are generally smaller, and many are self-contained. All equipment (facilities and IT) is inside the unit. These data centers may be in ISO shipping containers, modularly constructed from walls and panels manufactured offsite, inside office buildings, adjacent to cell towers, or even submerged below the ground for inner city deployments. Data centers in a box are gaining momentum for deployments with minimal compute needs.

Data centers in a box are devices that contain storage, networking, a server, and communications within a minimal footprint, literally, in a box or some stackable format. These devices, by design, operate with mostly remote administration. The housings protect the computing components from harsh environments. One may find these deployed at cellular sites or rural areas.

Edge computing and edge data centers support a wide range of services, but the expectation is that these will only grow in number and location. One use case is autonomous vehicles (AV). AV communications happen both inside and outside city limits. Another use case is agriculture, which uses various sensors for monitoring crops and herds. Leak detection for pipelines and monitoring for power line breaks utilize remote sensors. Likewise, these may communicate via edge data centers. The point is that there are and will continue to be data center jobs *everywhere*.

Supporting Building Areas and Miscellany

We are clearly discussing the data center area, but other supporting areas exist within the building envelope or site. In general terms, there will be areas for backup power equipment, including power conditioning and battery banks, cooling/heat rejection equipment, service corridors, and the data center floor as part of the data center. But that certainly isn't the totality of the building contents.

We discussed power briefly above, but the power equipment will be either on pads outside the data center, in air-conditioned rooms within the building, or perhaps in locations on the data center floor.

PUTTING IT ALL TOGETHER SO FAR   51

Figure 7. Example Data Center Floorplan

Outside the actual data center room, other supporting areas factor in planning. Other areas include:

- The **reception** area for visitors and receiving check-ins, badging, visitor instruction, and education is generally the first area inside the front doors. This area may have special needs like wall-mounted monitors, artwork, awards, or anything else the company wishes.
- **Office areas** for on-site personnel, vendors, and customers break/fix areas. Leased and consultant-run data centers have smart hands services. Smart hands are on-site technical resources are available to assist tenants and customers. Consultant-run facilities need office space for them.
- **Restrooms** should be located both inside and outside the secure area. Visitors should have access that doesn't require security badging.
- **Holding and receiving areas** should be off the data center floor. Equipment often comes in cardboard, which is dusty and flammable.
- **Staging areas and equipment** burn-in benches same as holding above, but this area will have desktop-level outlets, networking equipment, and likely moving carts with keyboard, video, and mouse components.
- **Media rooms** for optical, tape, or disk backup are environmentally controlled. Some tape libraries are on the data center floor, but it is more common for them to be in a separate room with fire suppression. Legacy tape systems are highly flammable.
- **UPS rooms** may be service corridors flanking the data center space. They may also be in separate purpose-built rooms. For redundancy purposes,

a facility may choose to have two rooms on opposite sides of the building. UPS equipment may also be on the data center floor; however, batteries are generally not allowed, as they are flammable and corrosive.

- **Battery rooms** flank the data center. The room(s) are tailored differently depending on the battery construction. For example, lithium-ion rooms look vastly different from lead-acid battery rooms.
- **Service corridors (SCs)** for air handling equipment generally flank the building. While not all data centers utilize them, these corridors provide an area where HVAC personnel can work on equipment without having to be on the floor with secure assets. This compartmentalization creates a layer of protection for security reasons. The corridor can also function as part of the air movement strategy.
- **Generators** may be in a room, under a roof, or outside. The type of generator, field conditions, number of generators, budget, and preference dictate environmental decisions. Sound levels are a factor. (They aren't always quiet.) Diesel generators connect to underground tanks. Natural gas generators will require access to gas lines. Exhaust requirements for interior installations are mandatory. If generators are located in the yard, fence the area.
- **Flywheels** use kinetic energy to create power. They have been in military use for some time. Flywheels are well-suited to outside conditions. However, in harsh environments, they may need some shelter. As they discharge rather quickly, they replace a UPS, not a generator.

- **Fuel cells** are another means of power generation. New fuel cell suppliers have entered the market, with some accepting orders two and three years in advance. For some time, fuel cells were only available by one company. Fuel cells may be implemented in series as primary or backup power. The units are roughly the size of a parking space. Some suppliers provide them via PPA or **Power Purchasing Agreement,** meaning that consumers pay for the power, but the supplier owns the fuel cells.
- **Meet-Me-Rooms (MMR)** are areas typically used by colocation facilities as an area for carriers to come in and data connections to leave via basket tray or ladder rack to individual data halls, suites, and cages. Think of them as carrier exchanges that the facility may or may not own. Several colocation providers operate exchanges and cloud onramps as a service to tenants. Often there are multiple carriers within the meet-me-room. Each carrier has a secure cabinet for its equipment and connectivity.
- **Telecommunications demarcation** areas and **entrance facilities** are where the carriers come into the building and may or may not be in a meet-me-room. Entrance facilities are typically on the exterior of a building and extended into the building for telecom use. Redundant paths should be on opposite sides of the building or a considerable distance apart to safeguard that no one can dig up both feeds.
- **Security room(s)** provide a space for security monitoring and personnel. Security is generally at the entrance or may be consolidated

into reception for admittance and monitored elsewhere.
- **Mantrap/People Traps and gates** are devices that trap a person in between two doors. Their purpose is to monitor ingress into the facility. Some have scales to catch people moving things out of the facility. Some are manned by armed security. In-building enterprise data centers don't generally implement them, but most shared tenant spaces do. The entrance only opens with the correct credentials.
- **Biometrics** often flank mantraps and gates. These systems are a perimeter security measure (sometimes carried inside to cages and cabinets) that allows people to unlock the device with fingerprints, iris scans, palm prints, facial recognition, etc.
- **Network Operations Centers (NOCs)** are the "transportation" monitoring brains of the facility. For more extensive facilities, this area looks a bit like the NASA command center. Monitors display technicians with the weather, health, power, PUE data, cooling efficiency, or any combination of monitoring information. Although uncommon, security monitoring may also be in this area. In most cases the **security operations center (SOC)** is self-contained and while it resembles the NOC with multiple monitors, the SOC is responsible for overall physical security operations and in some cases cybersecurity monitoring, although cyber may be in a separate area or included with the NOC.
- **Conference rooms** can be inside or outside of the secure area. In enterprise in-building data

centers, there will likely be other conference rooms. For colocation or wholesale facilities, and even some hyperscale facilities, the conference rooms are outside the secure area, so visitors don't need to pass complete security protocols for a simple meeting.
- **Storage areas** are separate from loading docks and staging. These are areas for storing consumables, supplies, spares, etc. This area should be secured.
- **ITAD (IT asset disposal)** areas are where technicians wipe data and applications from retiring equipment. Commissioning and decommissioning equipment is a critical part of ongoing operations. For sustainability reasons, an older kit can be refurbished and reused by others. The concept is known as **circular economy**. Sometimes, the equipment provides trade-in credit for new equipment but still needs to be wiped of any proprietary or personal information. This area may be separate for colocation facilities or part of the staging area where staff burns in and configures new equipment.

Engineers and CAD and 3D drawing drafters for civil, electrical, architectural, low voltage, and all the specialties engage in the early negotiations. Sometimes simple site drafts are extremely beneficial in sorting out areas and determining a site's advantages and deficiencies.

The Building Systems

As noted above, the building envelope refers to the walls, roof, and floor and includes water, heating and cooling, and light. The building envelope is supported by and through multiple systems and devices. The building is continuously monitored for fire, power drops, cooling, humidity, leaks, and efficiency, to name a few. Under the term building automation systems (BAS) or building management systems (BMS), these systems aim to assure constant environmental control. These networked systems may include HVAC, fire, security, lighting controls, and other integrated controllers, sensors, and system servers.

For example, lighting may follow a person walking down a hallway. The HVAC for an area may alter the temperature based on occupancy sensors. Windows may dim automatically during periods of direct sun. Data center heat rejection will ramp up during heavy compute periods. The idea is that the more you automate, the more efficiency is realized while decreasing the chances of human error.

IoT aka The Internet of Things

IoT refers to IP-connected devices of all sorts, including sensors. The more integrated the controls for the building are, the more intelligence is gleaned from the data and the more significant the benefits to the facility. While the core part of this exercise is examining the data center, personnel spaces will always be included. Integration of controls will consist of all areas, but each will have different environmental needs. Equipment comfort and people comfort are not the same. However, monitoring of these systems occurs via the controls equipment.

Monitoring via the NOC – Network Operations Center

Monitoring and health information feeds to the Network Operations Center (NOC). Sometimes environmental information is provided to a different area than the NOC. But, most often, it resides within the overall site monitoring. This specialized area is staffed by personnel trained to remedy problems or notify those who can. Typical NOCs have walls full of monitors, each with specific pieces of information about the ecosystem.

The NOC is responsible for monitoring the overall health of the ecosystem. Duties may include network and server monitoring or simply the facilities infrastructure (colocation). The NOC will interface with data center operations personnel for any fault or problem. They will also interface with data center and security personnel in the event of a fire, weather concern, or other life safety concern.

Sometimes, key information from the NOC is echoed in the reception area. Data centers like to advertise PUE, WUE, downtime, time without lost time accidents, etc.

The term "**single pain of glass (SPG)**" refers to having disparate systems populating information on a single screen for ease of use. Integrated systems and open systems allow SPG functions. In some cases, there may be some translating equipment necessary to facilitate SPG reporting.

POWER PARTICULARS

Sizing Power

Power needs understanding will help decide the amount of equipment supported and will vary based on the required redundancy. For the sake of this exercise, let's assume IT equipment and cooling need a total of 100kW of power for the primary service. (Note: This could be an actual number, an estimated number, or an assumed number for construction purposes and will generally be higher than 100kW.) Understanding what we learned above, simple primary power does not maintain uptime in the event of a failure. Adding battery backup and generators to this single power delivery method provides some backup. This backup power will last until battery capacity depletes or the generator runs out of fuel. It is more advantageous to have a secondary power supply for simple failures.

A simple power feed example follows:

Generator(s)
⇓
Utility Power ⇒ Switchgear ⇒ UPS ⇒ PDU ⇒ Equipment

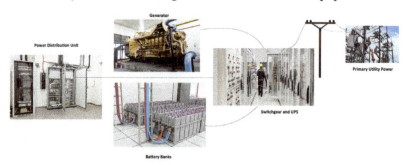

Figure 8. Power Delivery Feed for Primary Power
Note: Mechanical systems often have separate switchgear, but the feed is similar.

Back to our example, if the primary power required equals 100kW, backup generators must support 100kW in the most straightforward configuration. If backup power is live and inline, the primary is 100kW, as is secondary, for a total of 200kW of delivered energy. If only part of the data center uses secondary power, then the number will be somewhere between 100kW and 200kW. As shown in Figure 8, all components' generation capabilities are rated to support their respective loads. Higher draw facilities use multiple generators in series called gensets; spare gensets round out the redundancy requirements.

A UPS's size will match the power feed and supply backup power via the battery banks until generators or secondary power comes online. There are intricate calculations to determine the size of the UPS system. Considerations include power supplied and seconds of uptime needed. Temporary energy is not the only function of a UPS, however. UPSs also condition power by removing spikes and dips.

Data center power may be single-phase or three-phase. Three-phase distribution will result in higher efficiency. Additionally, brownfield sites may have limited power options. The act of distributing power generates losses. These losses cannot be engineered out of power distribution, but will undoubtedly factor into design considerations from conductor size to equipment.

Engineering is outside this book's scope, but electrical engineers are in great demand in the industry. Similarly, all of the power trades are in demand from equipment sales through installation and maintenance including electricians, journeyman, and apprentices.

Secondary Power and Failover

Secondary power is failover power to those systems that require constant uptime. As a matter of fact, secondary power is standard for larger data centers, colocation facilities, enterprise data centers, and other data centers. Secondary power normally equals main power by design, regardless of whether secondary power capacity is actively used. Centers achieve levels of power redundancy by doubling or tripling electrical components within the feeds. As mentioned previously, the highest level of redundancy is the most expensive for obvious reasons.

When the secondary power is there only in the event of a primary power failure, the power on the secondary side must equal the primary for all critical equipment. As such, the secondary power feed equipment mirrors the primary. For fault tolerance, the equipment and feeds are triplicated or quadrupled.

The concept of load sharing refers to primary and secondary power equally sharing the electrical demand of the equipment. For instance, a server may have a single power supply (primary) or two (primary and secondary). The server draws power from the primary power supply unless it fails which then flips to the secondary supply. With load sharing, it will use both. Likewise, servers, network switches, storage, and other equipment have dual power supplies. Load sharing is not available on all platforms.

Multiple components comprise the fault-tolerant design. Spares to the primary and secondary feeds come online as necessary. These inline components allow for any single feed's equipment to be maintained or taken offline without losing backup power services. One method of expressing redundancy is "N" or need.

N is simply the basic systems needed. N+1 is the system needed plus a spare. 2N refers to a fully redundant architecture where primary is mirrored to secondary and no manual intervention is needed to failover. One system can be worked on while the other is up and running.

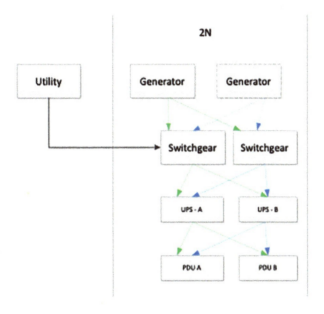

Figure 9. Example of Redundant Power Paths Common Configuration

Add additional power components for fault tolerance and concurrent maintainability, which is today's most deployed configuration. When a data center gets a rating/certification for redundancy (Tier, Category, etc.), the rating is based on both power and cooling redundancies. The lowest performing redundancy controls the rating number. For instance, if a data center is fault tolerant in power but not cooling, it will be rated lower than one with both fault-tolerant power *and* cooling.

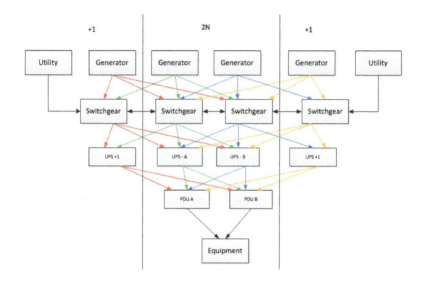

Figure 10. Example of Highly Fault Tolerant Design
The "N" noted is need.

AC versus DC

Conversion of power from AC to DC creates losses. The same is true for DC to AC. These conversions happen in several places along the power supply components. Utility power is AC; battery banks and active equipment operate via DC voltage. Active equipment takes in AC voltage and converts it to DC via the power supply to provide power to motherboards and the like. Where you measure power impacts the outcome of the measurements. If you measure only at the server, you ignore the losses and conversions along the way.

When measuring PUE in the purest form, utility power measured at the meter is best. However, that is not always possible. When power is on the same meter as the remainder of the building, it isn't likely to carve out the data center. The power meters won't break out into individual meters for individual cages within colocation facilities. Instead, intelligent PDUs (power distribution units) measure power from the inside delivery points to the endpoints.

The Open Compute Project utilizes DC power busways inside the cabinet for DC based compute in some of their designs. www.opencompute.org for more published designs and standards.

Power Monitoring and Stranded Power

Any power that is allocated and not used is known as stranded power. Currently, the data center industry estimates that 60–65 percent of distributed power is stranded. Work is needed to decrease this number. Part of the solution to stranded power is actively monitoring and managing the power within the facility. Using numbers from our example above, we can see the devastating costs and carbon burden of stranded power below. Bear in mind that these numbers do not include transmission fees or demand charges.

	Estimated Annual Power Cost	Annual CO_2 Emissions in Pounds for Natural Gas (898)	Annual Spend Coal	Annual CO_2 Emissions in Pounds/Coal (2180)
Total footprint	$ 399,568,916,400	51,210,784,800	$ 45,391,404,672	124,320,168,000
Average across markets	$ 28,540,636,886	3,657,913,200	$ 3,242,243,191	8,880,012,000
Waste @ 60% Stranded Power	$ 239,741,349,840	30,726,470,880	$ 27,234,842,803	74,592,100,800
Waste @ 65% Stranded Power	$ 259,719,795,660	33,287,010,120	$ 29,504,413,037	80,808,109,200

Figure 11. Understanding Stranded Power Costs

Power monitoring helps operations personnel understand power failures, fluctuations, the balance between power feeds, etc. Monitoring happens via software coupled with power infrastructure intelligence. We noted that there are often primary and secondary power feeds. If both power supplies from a server are plugged into primary power, then failover to secondary won't occur all due to simple human error. This type of scenario lessens with the use of monitoring software.

DCIM

Data center infrastructure management (DCIM) software is one such product. Most manufacturers of power equipment have some sort of management and monitoring software. Closed systems do not interface with other systems. Open systems do. When systems interface with each other, more actionable intelligence is possible. That is why some organizations prefer open DCIM systems over vendor-specific software.

Monitoring allows capacity planning decisions to be based on real-time data. This data should be actionable and not be data for data's sake. The extent of the data center monitoring depends on the various equipment capabilities, preferences, and organizational needs. Intelligent hardware comes at a premium over noncommunicating hardware. Remember the "you can't fix what you don't measure" statement from earlier? It certainly applies here. Many facilities operate as "lights out." Just as the name implies, they run without lights and people in them. Remote monitoring and control software allows many data center operations functions to be completed without stepping foot in the facility.

Once we know the power density of the site, we can divide the floor space into the appropriate number of rows. We also know enough to begin the selection of cooling solutions.

Density refers to the amount of equipment supported in a rack or across a row. The high-density designs may see support for 50-80kW per cabinet, while traditional passive designs are closer to 4-7kW per cabinet. This number represents the hard limit that can be supported without tripping a breaker.

The data room floor is designed based on various factors, but one of the most critical is the amount of power supplied per cabinet. Remember that the amount of power per cabinet will probably not be consistent across the data center floor during operation and may not be during design if the facility will implement some high-density areas. See whitespace design below for more.

COOLING AKA HEAT REJECTION

IT equipment generates heat. That heat must be removed. While technically, heat removal is the gist of the process, the process is still referred to as cooling industry-wide. As such, we will use that terminology here for simplicity. The development of cooling guidelines and directives for the data center falls under the guidance of **ASHRAE (American Society of Heating, Refrigeration, and Air-Conditioning Engineers)** in concert with active equipment manufacturers. These global standards set the recommended allowable operating temperature, humidity levels, and like parameters for the data center ecosystem. Any system can exceed these numbers, but the minimums are used for safe operating temperatures. When equipment overheats, not only does it shut down, nowadays it also records that event in sustainable memory and it will impact warranty claims.

Physics matter (always and sort of). Hot air rises, and cold air drops. However, air can be forced via fans just about anywhere. Physics can be manipulated by moving or forcing air. The trade-off is the power it takes to move the air or liquid. Cooling systems are installed with redundant components so that another unit can fill the demand if any unit fails. Some data centers are constructed with very high ceilings so that in the event of a failure, heated air rises far above active equipment. The thinking is that the ceiling will contain the hot air and there will be some time before the heated air is low enough to impact equipment.

Traditional total room cooling solutions adequately serve lower power densities up to about 5–7kW per cabinet. Newer mid-tier and hyperscale data centers drive higher power levels, 8kW–15kW and ultra high density 50–80kW per cabinet. At the highest densities, there is a need for either supplemental cooling, some type of containment (desirable regardless), immersion, rear door heat exchangers, on-chip liquid cooling, or other cooling methodology.

Types of Cooling

There are several means of cooling/heat rejection. We will discuss the cooling on the floor in the whitespace design section. Here, we are going to cover some of the equipment types. There are three ways to remove heat from a data center: air, water and other fluids, pumped refrigerants, or some combination. The idea behind them all is roughly the same. By absorbing the heat generated from the chips, we take the heated air or fluid and remove the heat, then move the cooler air to the air intake fans. The cycle continuously repeats.

Air conditioning refers not only to the temperature but also to the humidity levels. The equipment manufacturers and ASHRAE set recommended air inlet temperatures. Likewise, there are acceptable levels of humidity, measured in dry bulb temperatures, that must be maintained. These are explained in ANSI/ASHRAE Standard 90.4 (latest revision). Too little humidity and the room has too much static. Too much humidity and the room will have condensation. Neither are good friends with electronics. Note, higher elevation requirements vary from lower elevations.

Water is 3,500x better at absorbing heat than air. There are other refrigerants used that are also better absorbers than air. All have a place, but all do not share the same efficiencies. Selecting the right cooling technology depends on the power system's load density. Knowing the power draw for the space will determine the cooling needs, as there is a direct correlation.

HVAC service technicians are in great demand, particularly chiller technicians, controls technicians, etc. These skills are needed during and post construction for operations. MEP (mechanical, electrical, plumbing) drafters are in demand for designs, prefab configurations, Computational Fluid Dynamics (CFD) modeling, etc.

Some often-used cooling terms:

Condensers are the outside equipment portion of some chilling equipment housed in cabins. Condensors consist of coils, fans, a compressor to increase pressure, and controls.

Coils contain either water or fluids to draw in heat.

Fans circulate the air to and around the coils to foster heat transfer.

CRAC (computer room air conditioners) are passive solutions using mechanical cooling for the computer room. These solutions are effective at lower power densities. The unit is either on the data center floor or in corridors in the gray space that flanks the data center. CRACs can accommodate higher densities when closely coupled or paired with containment systems.

CRAH (computer room air handlers) work in concert with indirect cooling (see below) with coils and fans to move cool air where it needs to be. They may be on the data center floor or in corridors in the gray space.

How the heat transfer occurs, and the configuration of the cooling equipment varies. Key considerations include the amount of heat to be rejected, outside air temperatures, overall building needs, the density of equipment (power demand) within the facility, the data center's size, greenfield or brownfield, costs, and supply chain. Some companies with multiple facilities have different equipment at each. In addition, mechanical and electrical engineering firms may have preferences regarding the units they specify. Do your homework.

Heat Rejection Methods

Figure 12. Condensing units cooling towers

Evaporative cooling mechanisms are also known as adiabatic cooling. To understand the concept, it's perhaps easiest to give a real-world example. If you have been outside near a pool or water on a hot day, you notice that the air around the water is a cooler temperature, and the breeze off the water is cooler. If you submerge yourself in the water, the water absorbs your heat. When you get out, the air around you dries the droplets on your skin. Your body heat transfers to the water droplets. As the droplets evaporate, your body feels cooler.

The principles are the same for evaporative cooling in data centers, obviously without the pool. The heated air (directly through cooling pads or indirectly through fins and coils) meets and heats the water (or coolant fluid) as the water absorbs the heat. The heated water turns to gas at a higher temperature, evaporating as a gas outside through the condenser unit.

Sometimes cooling units reside on the data center floor. If they are in row or attached to the active equipment and electronics, the concept is known as **closely coupled**, meaning the cooling source is close to the heat source. The process is relatively the same, just closer to the heat source. Close-coupled cooling can be an excellent solution for high-density areas and, in some cases, is used for an entire data center. In others, cooling units are distributed across or around the data center floor.

"Free" air cooling filters, conditions, and introduces outside air into a facility. While it is generally referred to as free air, it isn't free to operate.

Figure 13. Free Air Cooling Example

Heated air expels via vents, fans, or mechanical equipment. Surprisingly, even scorching areas of the world benefit from outside air at least some part of the year. Make-up air (mechanical systems) maintains positive pressure within the space. The concept is to use the filtered cool air from outside as often as possible, while using units to provide the cooling (heat rejection) when the temperatures are outside of needed operating temperatures. Neighboring businesses should not be industrial with chemical exhausts or contaminants.

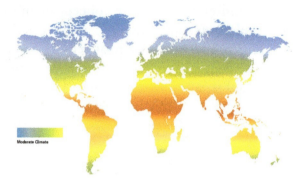

Figure 14. Photo courtesy of STULZ, Inc. – Climate Zones for Free air cooling

Direct evaporative cooling takes heated air and puts it in direct contact with water or fluid, absorbing the heat from the air. External direct evaporative systems that utilize cooling pads can use untreated water, while closed-loop systems require treated water.

Figure 15. Cooling Configuration Example

Indirect evaporative cooling works similarly, except the water and air do not come in direct contact. Instead, the water moves through coils via pumps. As this is a closed system, the water must be treated for microbes and devoid of corrosives, or the piping and coils will fail. If the system uses refrigerants, that fluid will be pretreated.

All systems have a marriage between the fan controls and water/fluid flow. More water is introduced to increase cooled air turnover, or the fans increase speed or both. Efficiencies will vary based on location, load, designs, and other factors. Increasing fan speed will remove more air, but the trade-off is higher power costs. Likewise, programming the controls and assuring the various systems communicate with each other for maximum room and heat rejection efficiency is critical.

DX (direct expansion) cooling uses refrigeration coils within the air stream. These units can be self-contained (sit on the floor) or whole building (package DX units) residing on the roof or adjacent to the building. Units can have fixed or variable speed fans that ramp up as needed. It is advantageous to have individual units communicate with each other for overall environmental control.

VRF (variable refrigerant flow) VRV (variable refrigerant volume) systems can control refrigerant flow as needed. For example, the refrigerant will increase refrigerant volume when more heat rejection is necessary.

Water Free Cooling uses air to reject heat. While this is a great solution for areas where water is at a premium, the trade-off is higher power bills as air is not as efficient as water in absorbing and rejecting heat. However, there are certainly locations where water is a scarce commodity. These solutions allow facilities to be built in those areas without concern for high water usage. Water usage effectiveness (WUE) is a metric that allows data centers to measure water similarly to PUE for power.

Controls systems are the controls attached to air handling and air moving equipment. They often communicate via TCP/IP. However, some systems use BACnet or MODBUS, requiring a gateway to communicate over TCP/IP with other IP-based systems.

On-Floor Cooling Systems Introduction

Figure 16. Servers submerged in non-dielectric liquid

Submersion is literal, as the name implies. Servers are submerged in a non-conductive liquid. There are two types of submersion technology, the main difference being that one traps and recycles vapors and the other does not. Submersion is a relatively new, promising technology with limited use to date. Submersion cooling shows great promise in both high-density applications and edge data centers. The Open Compute Project currently is working to add submersion cooling to their open data center designs.

COOLING AKA HEAT REJECTION 77

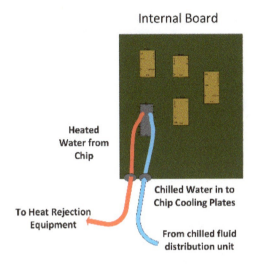

Figure 17. On Chip cooling

On-chip/Direct-to-chip cooling has piping systems fitted inside the cabinets that directly attach to the CPU processing chips via a cooling plate, or in some cases a cage. The extremely close-coupled cooling uses liquid piped through servers with a small unit attached directly over the chip. The fluid circulates as in the other systems carrying rejected heat to the external cooling system components. As the cooling fluid runs over the processors, the heat directly couples with the fluid. The heated fluid leaves via other piping tubes to the heat rejection equipment. This style allows for higher processing temperatures and can allow a facility to run 50-80kW per cabinet in some instances.

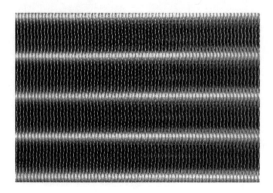

Figure 18. Rear door heat exchanger coils

Rear door heat exchangers operate like (and resemble) radiators attached to the rear of each cabinet. Cooled water or fluids circulate through the door's fins. The cooled fluid attracts the heat from the air egress on the back of a server, and heated water travels to external sources (more below). Again, as this is close coupled cooling, rear door heat exchangers allow data centers to design to higher equipment densities (more equipment per rack) while providing some energy efficiencies.

GRAY SPACE AND WHITE SPACE

Cooling units often flank the data center in service corridors called gray space.

The data center floor itself is called white space. This term is a throwback to the white tiles that cabinets used to occupy, although today, many facilities are built without raised floors. White spaces contain the IT active equipment. In some cases, remote power panels (RPPs), UPS units, cooling units, cooling distribution units, and other building infrastructure equipment are also deployed on the floor.

When designing cabinet positioning, pathways, and spaces for cables, walkways, and all on-floor and under floor (if a raised floor is used) assets, care must be taken to ensure that air handling systems operate in their optimal environments without obstructions to operations.

Fire Suppression

Figure 19. Fire Suppression Equipment

Fire suppression and/or sprinklers are a code requirement, and the local authority having jurisdiction should be consulted. Local codes can exceed the needs of the national building standards. Some fire suppression is required. In fact, insurance companies may also dictate what is used.

Fires can be caused by zinc whiskers, arc flash, overheating, dead shorts, dust, light fixtures, electrical systems, or other combustibles. Zink whiskers develop/grow over time on metals coated in zinc. They can break off and cause electrical shorts. Smoke detectors will be placed around the building and inside any contained aisles not equipped without breakaway ceilings.

Types of smoke detectors include:

- VESDA (Very Early Smoke Detector Apparatus)
- Ionization detectors (smoke ions create an electrical path setting off an alarm)
- Photoelectric (detection of light)
- Pressure bulb (bursts at 70C or higher)

Fire suppression systems can be wet or dry, with dry piped preferred. (No water is in the pipes until an event). Chemical systems are also available and include CO2 (not allowed in all places due to life safety concerns), Halon (grandfathered only), FM200/HFC-227, Inergen/IG-451, Argonite/IG55, Novec-1230, FE12-HVC23, and others. Each has pros and cons.

Some use chemical suppression first with additional heat sensors for the water to kick in if chemical suppression was not successful. Some facilities choose to use water (sprinklers) suppression only as they have full-time staff that could be the first responder for small events.

Sensors are required every 25 square meters (270 square feet) and must be one foot away from light fixtures.

Where fire suppression is used, the doors to the facility need to seal so that the suppression agent, under pressure, doesn't blow out the doors. As fire suppression is code related, it is always a good idea to work with an AHJ or fire design professional to be sure that the facility complies. Fire suppression designs are specialized and are another career opportunity along with installers, inspectors, AHJs, and others.

Penetrations and openings through fire rated walls, riser systems, and into adjacent areas must be filled with firestop materials. There are multiple types of firestopping materials and chases.

BIM -Building Information Management

Do an internet search on hyperscale data centers, and one can see the artistry built throughout the piping for cooling, fire, and other systems. During the design phase, it is important to glean an understanding of clearances, optimal conditions, and other systems that may impact pathways and pipe ways.

During the design and construction phase, one often used tool is **BIM. Building Information Management** models and software provide 3D representations of all components. It is invaluable to detect places where systems might interfere with each other before the build starts. In fact, with new virtual reality technology, one can do a virtual walk-through before any work begins. Drafters and designers are skilled trades heavily used in the design process. Civil, structural, mechanical, electrical, etc., drafters are all in high demand. Every equipment manufacturer and all design firms use drafters for BIM models and site designs.

Room Lighting

Many data centers utilize white, light gray, or beige cabinets to increase visibility. Black cabinets are better at hiding grime but absorb light and, as such, are difficult to see inside when working. Room lighting is critical to ensure that workers can see when working on equipment. Lighting should not be directly over cabinets but rather in the aisles. Light (measured in LUX) should minimally be as follows:

- Corridors - 200 lux min – recommended 300 lux
- Service areas – 150 lux min, 200 lux recommended
- Rooms min 500 lux, recommended 600 lux

Emergency lighting directing people to exits is **mandatory by code**.

Grounding/Bonding/Earthing

Code requires the installation of a telecommunications main grounding/bonding busbar. The busbar connects to the building earth/ground to eliminate any difference in potential. In addition, all metal components of the data center (pathways, racks, etc.), shielded patch panels (one end of the channel only), etc., shall be connected to the grounding system. (Note: Codes use the words shall and should but not interchangeably.) Shall is a mandate. Should is a strong recommendation but will not incur a fine if not followed.

There will likely be multiple telecommunications bonding busbars throughout the facility. Floor stanchions (if a raised floor is used) will all be connected to a bonding grid. This eliminates difference in potential and ground loops. Ground loops occur if a transient leaves one ground and re-enters the system via another ground. The idea is to provide a path of least resistance out of the building either through a single grounding conductor or through grounding conductors that have equalized potential to absorb (carry) the transient away from critical equipment.

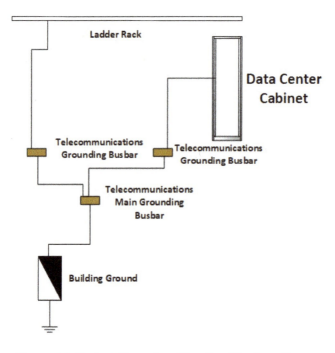

Figure 20. Typical Grounding/Bonding/Earthing System

Computational fluid dynamics (CFD) modeling is advantageous when planning high-density designs to model whether the heat will be rejected appropriately, and cooled air circulated correctly within the space without creating hotspots which would then require supplemental cooling. If you don't create a hotspot, you don't have to cool it. Sometimes, moving higher power equipment around the data center removes the need for high density areas.

It is wise to model any application outside the normative references for the supplier specifications. Modeling can pinpoint problems before the ill-sized equipment comes online, only to find later it was insufficient for the data center's needs. Some facilities update models frequently before equipment is purchased to ensure that it will operate as intended in the environment. There is a company that has tested literally every data center server in a variety of configurations that has built an amazing AI engine around picking the most efficient equipment. Tools like this can be invaluable.

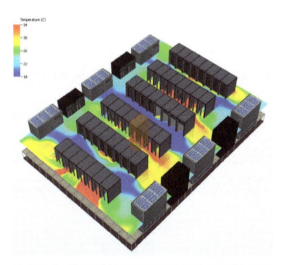

PHOTO CREDIT: DCIMNEWS.FILES.WORDPRESS.COM

Figure 21. CFD model of a data center floor

WHITE SPACE / GRAY SPACE DESIGN

Design for Longevity

In all areas, the data center isn't a short-term investment. The center will support multiple iterations of electronics and, as such, should be designed with the future in mind. Racks, cabling, power whips, and the like should have a long-installed life. Moves, adds, and changes are inevitable but carry costs and risks. In reality, the cabinets don't change. Instead, changes happen to the equipment inside. Typical lifecycles for active equipment vary from manufacturer to manufacturer, but data centers generally refresh their active components (servers, switches, storage, etc.) every three to five years. As sustainability becomes more of a decision factor, some companies keep their equipment as long as seven years or until a manufacturer announces end of life for that gear.

Capital equipment (power, cooling, infrastructure) components have significantly longer lifespans with proper maintenance. Most of this equipment depreciates over time making replacement before full depreciation difficult at best due to tax recapture burdens.

Downtime

Downtime is a risk. Part of any design is determining risks and justifying the costs to avoid them. When a data center goes down for any reason, work stops. Therefore, downtime costs in the data center are far greater than, for instance, if one user loses a laptop. Some downtime costs are tangible; some are not.

If there is an outage, users can't work, the company will likely lose revenue, and its reputation will suffer. If the data center happens to be a colocation or cloud facility, the impacts exacerbate further, as multiple companies are affected. For this reason, the latter generally have SLAs (service level agreements) in place to monetarily protect tenants during an outage. The higher uptime required, the higher the fees for the space.

Some cloud applications operate on a "best effort" basis. Carefully negotiate based on actual risk. Although estimates say that if one read all end user license agreements they come in contact with in their life it would take 13 years on average, this is not a time to skip that important step.

Sample justifications may look like the following:

- Number of users x weighted salary = salary cost of unproductive time
- Revenue / # of employees / 2080 = hourly revenue burden per employee (use total employees)
- Salary burden + revenue burden x hours down = internal downtime costs

Colos and cloud facilities burden will be cumulative results from each tenant's total. MMTR (mean time to repair) estimates are available from most manufacturers and help with duration calculations. Average downtime costs for a data center are estimated to be $5,600 per minute, although industry estimates vary widely. The point is downtime is expensive!

Companies spend vast amounts of money on redundancy and resiliency to avoid those costs. Many have alternative suppliers on speed dial to handle supply chain problems. Some chose to have one manufacturer at one site with others at other sites to mitigate supply chain risks. Supply chain can impact any step from construction through operations.

Labor is also a consideration for any installation in the space. Labor to install is a given at the outset. Avoid equipment and labor costs associated with ripping out and replacing equipment whenever possible. With abatement and removal, there may also be fees associated with recycling. When running calculations comparing solutions, be sure to think long term.

General Whitespace Design Considerations

The data room floor is designed based on multiple consideration factors, but one of the most critical is the amount of power per cabinet. Bear in mind that the amount of power per cabinet will probably not be consistent across the data center floor during operation and may not be during design. The reason that the amount of power per cabinet is critical is due to the following:

- Planning equipment placement
- Planning power and cooling capacity
- Planning any power load sharing
- Determining what equipment will have primary and secondary power
- Designing the power distribution systems and assuring that the right equipment (floor distributors, breakers, remote power panels, and power backups) can carry the load
- During operations to ensure there will be enough power and cooling capacity in the room
- Determining the amount of active equipment that any cabinet can support
- Assuring circuits do not get overloaded and fail

Airflow Considerations

Airflow within the cabinets is designed so that cold air gets pulled in through the perforated doors in front of the cabinet into the intakes of the active equipment by internal fans. As the air crosses the chips, it picks up the heat generated by the chips and exhausts the heated air through the rear of the cabinet. Standards-based airflow is front to rear, front to top, or front to top and rear. Unfortunately, although rare, there is equipment out there that does NOT follow the standards, and it is crucial to determine the airflow of the equipment or specify the expectations. Thankfully, non-standard equipment is becoming scarcer.

Cool air arrives at the cabinet front from under a raised floor, adjacent from in-row air equipment, or from above. Hot air can be ducted from the equipment air exhaust at the rear of cabinets into a plenum above the ceiling or simply drawn into the heat rejection equipment via its placement facilitating air draw.

The difference in the intake and exhaust temperatures is called the delta-T (Δ-T). Heat rejection equipment works more efficiently with a higher Δ-T. Simply put, the efficiency is greater when it rejects more heat than it would be with just a couple of degrees. Computer room air conditioners (CRACs) and computer room air handlers (CRAHs) work to circulate air within the space. Depending on the equipment used, these units can serve the room, a row, or a few cabinets.

The power density will impact the choices for heat rejection equipment. Workloads may require equipment with very different power characteristics. To deal with widely varying workloads and power demands, some data centers will use distinct areas that support high density (i.e., 25kW racks) and others supporting low density (i.e., 5–7kW racks) equipment.

Some DCs are built to higher density specifications everywhere. Horizontal density distribution refers to multiple lower power cabinets, while vertical density refers to fewer cabinets with higher delivered power. Each will have unique design requirements.

Once the facility moves to operations, the cabinets will have varying power draws as loads fluctuate. A wise facility measures power constantly and understands the changing demands. The best designs integrate cooling into the power monitoring for overall capacity planning.

High-density areas: As noted above, some DCs utilize the maximum power per cabinet in fixed areas instead of designing the entire room for high power. So, in effect, there would be a high-density area (i.e., 25kW per cabinet) and maybe some low-density rows of 5–7kW. The overall traditional cooling in the room would not be able to handle 25kW cabinets. In this case, some other means of supplemental cooling will be necessary for that higher-density area. Overloading a cabinet on the floor with too much equipment, even if the power is available, creates a hot spot (or spots). Hot spots lead to equipment failure.

While it may seem wise to just design the whole building for higher density, it is essential to note that not all facilities can support an overall high-density design. Likewise, waste is expensive. Upstream power, space for backup power equipment, existing site conditions, budget restrictions, etc., may limit power supplied. Greenfield designs are not as limited with proper site selection. Hyperscalers and facilities designed with high-density needs require more land for supporting systems (see site selection above).

On the Floor

Cabinets are placed in rows on the floor in a hot aisle/cold aisle arrangement (Figure 23), with the front of two cabinets facing each other (cold aisle) and the rear of two cabinets facing (hot aisle). The arrangement keeps the hot air from one cabinet from becoming the intake air of the next row.

The separation of hot and cold air is a critical efficiency booster. Containment systems stop the air missing around the end of rows. Blanking panels (blank out open spaces) stop air from mixing inside cabinets.

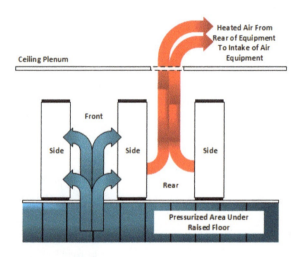

Figure 22. Traditional Raised Floor Passive Room Air

Cold air enters the room through cold aisle perforated or grated tiles. Tiles can be enhanced with fans for increased airflow. The equipment discharges the heated air out the rear. The heated air moves to the ceiling (plenum or open) where it is drawn into the equipment as noted above.

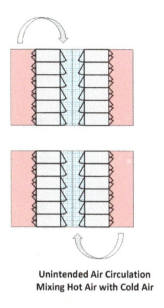

Unintended Air Circulation
Mixing Hot Air with Cold Air

Figure 23. Typical Aisle Arrangement (Top View)

Aisle Containment Systems

To gain energy efficiencies, row containment provides an effective solution for separating hot and cold air. Room air moves up when forced from beneath a raised floor (Figure 22) or dropped from above without a raised floor. In-row cooling units provide adjacently forced air. Containment systems provide a sealed corridor for either the hot aisle, the cold aisle, or both. Containment systems can use room cooling, or close coupled cooling within the row. However, there remains a great debate within the industry as to which is better. Proponents of the hot aisle containment (HAC) believe that containing heated air is a better solution (Figure 25), and the proponents of the cold aisle (Figure 24) think conversely. Both have their evangelists. Some facilities do both HAC and CAC.

Figure 24. CFD - Cold Aisle Containment

Due to existing computer room conditions, brownfield containment installations differ slightly from greenfield. The overall room design and existing equipment configurations may show one to be less expensive and disruptive than the other. The overall return on investment (ROI) of each solution needs investigation. Due to the fire suppression within the space—lighting, air movement, ceilings, plenums, etc.—hot aisle containment may be more advantageous. In contrast, it may be less costly to contain the cold aisle in other data centers.

The air equipment should not be so strong that air is sucked through the equipment faster than it can pick up the heat from the processors. This effect is called the Venturi effect. As a result, the air blows by without benefit.

From a design perspective, either HAC or CAC works to separate hot and cold air. Often, the choice between them is simply a preference. Containment systems consist of curtains or doors for each end of the aisle, a ceiling for the cold aisle, or ducting for the hot air into the ceiling space (plenum) in the hot aisle. In addition, all air gaps within the cabinets need outfitting with blanking panels. Hot and cold will mix within the cabinet just as it mixes within the room. The contained aisle acts as a corridor.

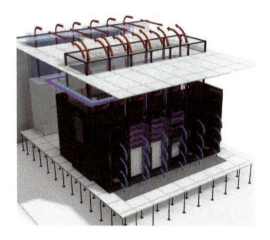

Figure 25. Hot Aisle Containment

Hot air is contained and channeled to a ceiling grate or into the ceiling where the CRAC intake is also ducted. The hot aisle containment system acts as a duct into the ceiling area keeping the heated air from the room. The hot aisle can also be directly ducted into the air handling equipment, although this is costlier, it does keep the hot air from mixing with room air before it enters the air equipment. The diagram above shows such a chimney system. This same concept can also work with in row cooling equipment (below).

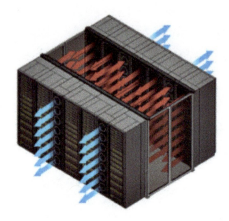

Figure 26. In Row Cooling with Hot Aisle Containment

Hot air could also be drawn into the rear of in-row air units. These units are connected to chilled water or refrigerant systems. Chiller distribution units move the liquid to external chiller or cooling components for heat rejection.

Figure 27. Cold Aisle Containment

The opposite principle is cold aisle containment (CAC) above. In this case, the cold aisle is the corridor allowing cold air to circulate to the top of the cabinet positions. Hot air discharges to the room. Room units or in-row cooling units supply the cold air.

As a side note, it is crucial to design the fire suppression systems so that the entire room (including under any containment ceiling) has coverage by suppression. Aisle ceilings can break away, retract, or additional suppression heads are needed. In some cases, cabinets contain in-cabinet fire suppression. In all cases of fire suppression, the AHJ (Authority Having Jurisdiction) should be included, as sometimes local ordinances go above and beyond the National Building Codes and National Electrical Code. Failures to either code can result in a denial of a certificate of occupancy, fines, or both.

It's always a good idea to check the manufacturers' specifications to ensure you can reject the right amount of heat for your environment. In some cases, data centers operate multiple solutions, one for high-density areas and the other for lower-density areas. Some colocation facilities will have manufacturer-specific requirements for what types (and, in some cases, manufacturers) can be installed in their data halls. Rigid specifications are limiting factors with design constraints.

For colo environments, the facility engineering outlines detailed power ratings used for sales and ongoing management purposes. Operating outside of these specs requires additional engineering and coordination and time. Leasing for data halls may include an entire suite/hall. Leasing may be for smaller areas generally configured in cages acting as mini data halls. In some cases, colocation facilities will lease out portions of racks.

Raised Floor or Not?

This question is another ongoing debate within the industry. Both raised floor and on slab designs exist in data centers. In general, the raised floor acts as an air plenum if CRAC units utilize the space for air delivery. As such, components installed in that plenum space need to follow the plenum codes for the respective county. If it doesn't serve air, it is still conducive to piping, high voltage, low voltage, fiber, etc., without plenum restrictions. Any of these services not put under a raised floor are located overhead.

Cold aisles are fitted with perforated or grated tiles that allow the air to flow up through those tiles while the remainder of the room is solid. The area under the raised floor is pressurized. The static pressure under the floor helps control airflow and air direction. Units have different capacities to pressurize that area. There are requirements for perforated tiles and how much of the floor they can occupy. One should not put perforated tiles where they are not needed.

It is critical that in these environments, any opening that isn't providing chilled air to equipment on a raised floor is sealed with air pillows or gaskets to maintain this static pressure and assure that the cold air is only escaping where it is required.

There are some other advantages to a raised floor. Plumbing can be located there, effectively putting the equipment and power above any minor leakage. Be sure to install moisture sensors and monitoring. There is a variety of cooling equipment for raised floor environments. Some use the raised floor for air delivery; some do not.

The airflow must be unobstructed when utilizing the space for air delivery. The pathways below the floor will generally run parallel to the cabinets. For trays that need to run perpendicularly for row-to-row connectivity, the perpendicular pathways route through the center of the room when CRACs/CRAHs flank both sides. When CRAC/CRAH units are on one side, perpendicular trays run at the far end, providing unobstructed airflow. Proper separation and isolation between systems is necessary if multiple systems exist under the raised floor.

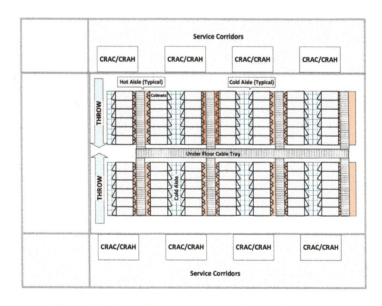

Figure 28. Cable Tray Routing for Under Floor Area

Any unit's throw is the distance the CRAC's/CRAH's fans can push the air. The unit's throw is a critical factor in passive room designs (where the entire room is cooled). Locate cabinets leaving space in front of the CRAC units for maintenance. Cabinets placed too close to air handling equipment will be bypassed by cold air due to the force of the air. It takes the air a little distance to slow down enough to move through a tile.

Although rare, a raised floor can also be used simply as a floor without any underlying systems. The open area under the floor is available for power, low voltage pathways, other piping (separate from any voltage source and install leak sensors), or some combination, provided there is adequate clearance. A raised floor should be at least 16 inches (41cm), although 24–36 (.5 to 1m) is preferred. Some facilities (colocation in particular) may have to install dams or fences/partitions below the raised floor to protect from unauthorized access to adjacent cages. Some pros and cons of a raised floor are listed below.

Raised Floor Pros	Raised Floor Cons
Provides an area for air, pathways, and piping	Cost of the floor (even higher in seismic areas)
Well understood from a design perspective	Weight loading will likely be less than concrete
Provides a means to isolate leaks	May require sprinklers under the floor
Works well with hot or cold aisle containment	Maintenance tile removal restrictions apply. Removing too many tiles may cause floor failure.
Antistatic floor, no special concrete treatment needed	It may require more costly plenum cable (North America)
Workers do not need ladders if pathways are under floors	Workers will need to be on ladders above active equipment for moves, adds, and changes
Easier remediation of pathways	Additional considerations for modular scalability with room CRAC/CRAH units
Easy to use as a grid for identification and spacing	Floor voids must be cleaned and remain uncluttered
Moves, adds, and changes to the infrastructure below do not require a ladder	Overhead pathways are more difficult to clean.
The grounding grid equalizes potential and is available for other grounding needs	Requires separate grounding/bonding pathway system connections
Allows isolation of some systems	Requires leak detection if used for plumbing and separation from power conductors

The void under a raised floor must not be used for storage. Also, the entire data center, including the void under the floor, should be cleaned with HEPA filters at least once yearly. There are companies that do this sort of service, and most jobs are suitable for veterans or non-degreed folks starting out in the industry. It's a great way to get started.

General Rack/Cabinet Considerations

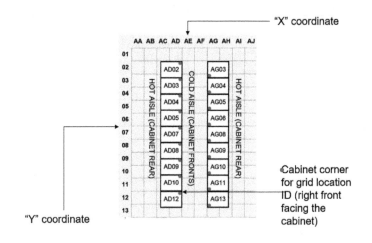

Figure 29. Grid Showing Floor Locations for Cabinets

One other advantage of a floor system is the grid layout naturally helps identify cabinets and rows. Data centers without raised floors often still use grid locations to identify cabinets. Cabinet labels are displayed on the cabinet front and grid locations are displayed along the walls.

For cabling, the patch panel or fiber port at one end is referenced by the location of the opposite end. This way, when someone is working inside a cabinet, they don't have to trace the channel to see what is at the other end. Regardless of whether a facility uses the grid method or simply names cabinets, adhering to labeling norms is helpful for installers and ongoing operations. Labeling is imperative for ease in troubleshooting.

Cabinet Considerations

Data center cabinets can vary in size, but a data center cabinet generally is 48 inches (1.2m) deep with 19-inch mounting rails. Mounting rail distances are standard across most cabinets. Standard data center racks and cabinets can range from 42RU up to 60RU. A rack unit (RU) is 1.75 inches (4.4cm) and applies to both open racks and cabinets. These two terms are sometimes used interchangeably. Technically racks are open frames without doors. Cabinets are enclosed. But know that not everyone adheres to that definition, using the terms interchangeably.

Note that the elevator and other clearances may limit usable cabinet height. Cabinets assembled on-site provide relief from clearance issues but add to installation time. Additionally, some seismic areas do not allow using non-welded (constructed on-site) cabinets. For seismic-rated locations, some data centers deploy shifting pads/iso pads that absorb movements to protect equipment and cabling. Always check seismic requirements before designing any space.

Networking and storage area racks may be (and should be) wider to accommodate the volume of network cabling required. Cabling must be able to be dressed so that it does not block the air intake of the active electronics (servers, routers, switches, etc.), remain dressed, and not introduce the risks associated with cable spaghetti. Without proper cable management, accidental disconnects can occur. In addition, cables can be pinched or crushed, destroying their performance. Room for the cabling plant is often under designed. If the cabling is substandard for any reason, the network performance will suffer or fail.

The cold aisle side of the cabinet will have vented air openings, and the percentage of air that enters varies by manufacturer. The hot aisle may be solid or vented. If hot aisle containment or room cooling is used, they are vented. For cabinets with a solid rear door, chimneys direct the hot air through the top of the cabinet to the ceiling plenum. The chimney is ductwork from the top of the cabinet like the chimney in a hot aisle, but cabinet width and specific, extending into the ceiling plenum. Chimneys are losing favor to hot aisle containment configurations but still have a purpose in some applications. Brownfield installation will probably stick with the same design when expanding.

The spacing of the aisles behind and in front of cabinets must be sufficient to allow equipment installation and removal. Larger equipment installations use server lifts requiring adequate clearances. In some countries, there are life safety considerations for hot aisles, which may sway a design to a cold aisle configuration.

Cabinets will be equipped with rack PDUs (power strips) to distribute power within the cabinet. Rack PDUs should be sized based on power design parameters. There will be one for primary and one for secondary in most configurations. Power distribution to the PDUs could be in the form of busways, power whips from remote power panels, on-floor larger PDUs, or a combination in some older facilities as explained earlier. Some owners/occupants prefer to use the raised floor for power. Some chose to put high/medium voltage under the floor and low voltage (structured cabling) above the cabinets or vice versa.

Figure 30. In cabinet PDU with primary and secondary power connections.

It's advantageous to preselect cabinets and power routing before the whitespace layout starts. Power knowledge is needed to determine the number of cabinets and density—both power and cabinet selections factor in cooling decisions for the room. Likewise, room cooling may impact cabinet selection.

For example, suppose a decision to use passive (total) room cooling occurs. In that case, one will want to be sure that the cabinets have the correct amount of perforation in the front doors. For in-row cooling and containment, leave spaces for the cooling units between cabinets as needed. Power draw requirements (designed or actual) must be known to determine the quantity and sizing for air units. If the facility design accommodates around 4kW per cabinet, it is unlikely that any cabinet will get filled with equipment. Therefore, one will not want the tallest cabinets available. As you can see, many of the decisions for the build are intertwined. Overbuilding is wasteful and expensive both to build and operate.

GENERAL INFORMATION – ACTIVE EQUIPMENT

GENERAL INFORMATION – ACTIVE EQUIPMENT 107

The third component of the trinity for data centers is the active equipment that lives in the cabinets and racks across the floor space. As we have learned, the equipment, power, and cooling go hand in hand. If one plans for equipment across a brownfield, two of those factors are already in place, and the remaining equipment placement on the floor must respect the limits of the room. If areas require more power than is offered, additional feeds from a provider or other source will be needed. If the room cooling can't support the heat rejection, some other design will be needed there, too.

The servers will generally share keyboard, video and mouse (KVM) devices or be administered remotely over the network.

Servers

Figure 31. Server wall

There are several types of servers from which to select. As they are sometimes known, pizza box servers get their name as they are typically 1 or 2 rack units (RUs) and resemble the box (minus the enticing pizza aroma). Some servers are 3–4RU or greater. Larger chassis-based servers are multiple RUs with individual blades that fit into slots within the chassis. These blade servers may have internal networking switches. Servers may or may not have hard drives for internal storage and operating systems.

To be a server, any of the above boxes need an operating system to boot, an application to run, memory to support the configuration, and disks to store application data. That storage may be on an internal disk, an external storage array (covered later), cloud-based storage, or any combination of the above.

Figure 32. Blade Server with Inserted Server Blades

Virtualization refers to multiple servers that operate over a single physical hardware platform. Virtualization allows multiple servers to *act* as though they singularly controlled the hardware. Still, CPU, memory, power, and sometimes networking resources are shared among all servers residing on the hardware. Virtualization allows some applications to use the lull of other applications for maximum server efficiency. Servers are segmented from each other by software.

For example, Company A has a payroll package on a server. The payroll processes twice a month. For the remaining time, that server draws power, adds heat to the environment, and utilizes network resources without benefitting the organization. But, if the organization uses the leftover time and resources from another server, both applications operate as if standalone, but via a single hardware. The fact that the server is not tied to the hardware in a 1:1 configuration is referred to as abstraction. However, applications are sophisticated enough these days to share hardware resources. This idea of hardware sharing, coupled with knowledge of mainframe environments, led to cloud computing. To put this in a frame of reference, consider running multiple applications on a laptop. Now we know that the laptop has one operating system (Windows, Linux, IOS). But if the office application, and the email application, and a streaming application were virtualized, they wouldn't operate over the same operating system. They would operate over copies of the operating system and any one's failure wouldn't bother the remaining instances.

Example of Server Sizing

Existing data centers have historical data to help to determine the number and size of servers. Institutions can predict growth based on past performance or some industry knowledge. However, in the case of a brand-new company or new venture, figuring out the size and number of servers without any experience is daunting. While it may seem prudent to rely on vendors and equipment manufacturers for guidance, the news is full of cases where that didn't work out so well. Due diligence matters.

The number of servers needed depends on the application(s) needs, amount of processing, RAM (random access memory), concurrent users, etc., in each server. One planning key here is concurrent users. Assuming a server application will span at least four time zones (mainland USA), it is safe to say that not all suggested users will be on simultaneously. Also, even in the same time zone, not all people will be on at the same time.

For example, a pizza chain sells an average of 3 million pizzas a day (1.5 million in the US), and there are 34 million unique combinations for their pizzas. Seventy percent of those sales were digital. So right off the bat, we know that not all customers use their application. They are calling instead.

The pizza chain has 5,992 stores in the US alone. If we assume each store has 2,000 customers, 2,000 x 5,992 = 111,984,000 unique customers.

If they sell 1.5m pizzas daily in the US, 1.5 x 365 = 547,500,000 each year (that's a lot of pizza). 547,500,000 / 111,984,000 = ~5. So roughly five pizzas per unique customer per year.

It becomes clear in this example that users only hit the site an average of five times per year to order, and we may assume five times per year to look and not order.

Driving factors for server sizing will be as follows:

- Simultaneous user expectations
- Number of processing cores
- Storage throughput (the ability to store and retrieve orders in this case)
- Storage for retention, past purchasing habits, customer information, etc.

- RAM or DRAM to run the application and provide faster memory processing

It's important to note that any application will (and must) scale. That is, the environment will grow with the user base. The choice might include one web server for the application for some number of users and one server for the database, or there may be a separate scalable storage array. Generally, a single CPU core can handle about 220–250 users. Servers can have more than one core. Make and list all assumptions.

All data center design must conform to the power requirements of the room. Assumptions can change as the design evolves, but it is a starting point. Engage the systems engineers (another job) from the hardware company or utilize a product that has already modeled server performance. Server selection and sizing software based on lab testing of most server brands and configurations on the market may be a wise investment. This software can look at existing data center assets and recommend cost-effective solutions in a vendor-agnostic manner.

When the application deploys, there will be a beta period where you can tell if your assumptions hold true. There should always be a growth factor that you can pull into the initial phase if throughput/performance is not what you expect.

A single hardware server can run multiple software servers. Once a company determines the operating system(s), manufacturer guidance regarding size, number of cores, and servers per hardware box provide other valuable pieces of input. Cloud configurators may provide some sizing metrics.

Servers will carry a nameplate rating for the power supply. A nameplate rating is a safety number; roughly

65 to 70 percent of that rating is actual consumption. Most server manufacturers will supply power utilization requirements based on various configuration options— *use them*. Ask, however, if the number is modeled or tested. Tested numbers are most useful, but modeled numbers provide guidance.

When working with existing or new equipment, it is critical to verify that the draw of servers within a cabinet does not exceed the power supplied to it to avoid failures. Ongoing, beneficial intelligent PDUs allow remote administration and reporting from individual ports. When intelligent PDUs integrate into DCIM or other power management software, management of real power is possible and encouraged! Data center operations personnel use these models to control capacity and plan positioning of on floor assets.

NETWORKING AND CABLING BASICS

Networking General Information

Like our highway system, networking defines how machines communicate, how fast they communicate with one another, and how users will communicate with the server applications. Servers, storage devices, firewalls, and wide area network (WAN) devices communicate via networks. The standard languages they use for communications are called protocols.

Conversations are divided up and put into packets for delivery. The packets are numbered at creation so that the receiving communications device can reassemble them. If any packet fails, for whatever reason, packet loss occurs. Lost packets must be retransmitted for the conversation to be understood. Unfortunately, too many retransmissions create unnecessary traffic. Ill-performing cabling channels are major culprits of retransmissions.

Networking is wired or wireless; both require uplink cables. Wireless devices connect to a wired switch. Wired connections utilize copper and fiber as communications media. Server networking connections generally come in pairs, one to primary and one to secondary networks, known as **resiliency**. Sometimes, a management network separate from the communications network is used for monitoring and management. This independent network is referred to as an out-of-band network. Out of band networks provide a layer of security by segmenting management traffic and also allows for access if the main network fails for any reason.

Most data centers consist of wired networks, although wireless may be available to assist with troubleshooting telephone calls and near-range inventory tracking. Many data centers intentionally do not allow wireless.

Wired and wireless networks intercommunicate via a common language (TCP/IP) used globally. TCP/IP is the language of the Internet, and all connected communications equipment understands it. Voice, video, streaming, and application communications natively speak TCP/IP, or their payloads (data) can be encapsulated within TCP/IP packets.

TCP/IP (transmission control protocol/Internet protocol) is a suite of instructions that include how to connect, where to connect, what device is next in line to pass information to, and how long to live (bounce around devices) before the packet drops, just to name a few functions. It also contains information databases (domain name servers - DNS) that tie addresses to names. For example, typing www.anything.com will translate the words to a number. The number corresponds to a server. Devices called routers, well, route the request to the server. The server then sends back the requested content.

Networking is a career itself. We won't dwell on it here. But a basic understanding is excellent for anyone to have. Routers work at the edge of any network to connect to the Internet. The router is responsible for routing the traffic to the next device, known as a hop. The Internet is smart enough to get a packet from one place to another in either the lowest number of hops or the least congested route based on the intelligence in the connected electronics.

Example:
Suppose you wish to login to a video website.

- First., you send a request to the server via your application.

- The internet translates the www address to a numerical address. The packet gets routed over the internet to a server (similar to a postal address).
- The request begins a connection (very similar to making a phone call). That request is routed to the server to say, "Hey, I want a connection."
- The server then sends back a form for you to fill in your login information.
- After filling in the username and password, the data returns to the server.
- The server compares your credentials with its database to see if you are "OK to browse."
- Once authenticated (user ID and password are accepted), the server tells your application that you can search for available content and view it.
- The packets that contain the videos return to you via the communication link established.
- Your phone decodes the packets and voila! The videos are displayed. When you hit buttons like fast forward, rewind, etc. you are actually sending commands to the server.

The application is responsible for formatting the videos for you to see. When the Internet is slow, or there isn't enough bandwidth for the application, it is easy to notice the slowdown (the dreaded spinning circle).

Following the above example, the server is fetching video data from storage devices (see storage below). The data center may contain separate storage and/or backup networks, or the storage disk may be inside the physical server case. Sometimes, the server has an internal drive to boot up and load operating systems and virtualization software, but the database that stores application information lives in the storage array.

Storage Networking

Storage arrays are typical. Arrays are multiple discs grouped for use by servers. The concept is analogous to filing cabinets. One can think of the hard drive as a file and the storage array as a room of filing cabinets. Permissions govern access to files.

Figure 33. Storage Array

Most communications networks utilize TCP/IP and Ethernet for connectivity. However, sometimes storage area networks (SANs) communicate via Fibre Channel on a disparate network. Fibre Channel is a standard that covers the communications, media (copper or fiber), storage area switches, and of course, disk arrays. Fibre Channel packets get encapsulated into TCP/IP for Internet routing. Devices called gateways act as translators between two different protocols. The easiest way to visualize this is to think of a translation application. The conversations are translated in both directions. There is a minimal amount of time added for the translation.

The number of networks within any data center is a design consideration. Separating traffic can alleviate or mitigate bottlenecks (choke points). Most networks in data centers today address both north/south traffic (that traffic that goes in and out of a data center) and east/west traffic (communications between servers, storage, and other communications equipment that never leaves the data center).

Networking and Communications

All cabinets have connectivity to network services via copper or fiber or, most often, both. Each cabinet uses the appropriate pathways and spaces above (or below) to ensure that cabling channels follow manufacturer and standards' installation specifications. The choices between copper and fiber consider the following:

- End-user preference
- Cost of electronics
- Power consumption
- Port utilization (unused ports can be wasteful)
- Distance supported (this is a hard limit)
- Switch configuration
- Application requirements (no pesky bottlenecks)

In the illustration below, you will see a Logical network layout. The core switch is in the middle and communicates to the other switches. Data centers can also operate via one or a pair of core switches. Manufacturers will help with your configuration. However, one should do their due diligence to ensure purchasing the proper hardware/port balance without overbuying. Endpoints on the below diagram are either servers, other locations, or end-user machines. The core of this network is fully meshed (fault tolerant). That is, no one outage will bring it all down. (The visual of a mesh network is a pretty good visual for the Internet).

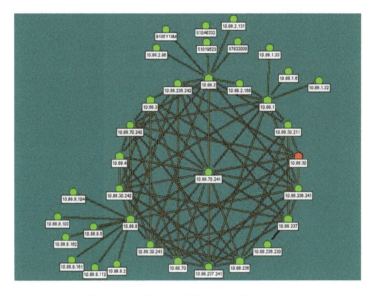

Figure 34. Logical Network Diagram

Traffic is not steady on most networking interfaces. Ethernet activity happens in bursts. Imagine a group of people. Not everyone talks at once. Most of the time spent in the crowds is spent listening, formulating thoughts, etc. People only speak when they have something to say. Networking traffic is the same.

The local area network (LAN) within the data center processes about 80 percent of the overall traffic internally (known as east-west traffic). Local communications include servers talking to storage, other servers, backups, making sure their resilient components are live, etc. Traffic leaving the data center (aka north-south traffic) only accounts for about 20 percent via the wide area network (WAN) or out to local users. Meaning one doesn't have to assume one Internet port for each server. Instead, we assume that servers will share the network with other servers.

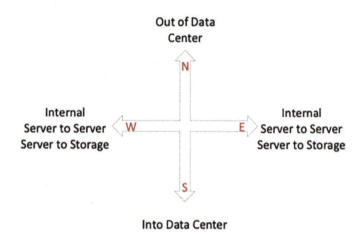

Figure 35. East West Traffic versus North South

You need to select networking speeds and port density based on concurrent users. Server side (east-west) traffic reads and writes to storage and equipment inside the data center; again, traffic won't be continuous nor full-time.

IEEE is the organization that governs standards for Ethernet, and they liaise with TIA and ISO/IEC for the physical medium (copper and fiber) standards. The Fibre Channel industry governs Fibre Channel storage. Therefore, if one uses Fibre Channel over Ethernet (FCoE), the storage communications will happen over the same networking interface as the Ethernet network.

Fibre Channel packets are "stuffed" into IP packets for transmission. Infiniband is another storage protocol and governed by the Infiniband Trade Association.

Ethernet Speeds and Media

Networks have multiple speeds available. In addition, equipment network attachments likely have both primary and secondary networks for failover resiliency. Backbone/uplink connections are higher speed than the port connections for equipment. A typical configuration may have a 32-port switch with 1 gig ports to servers and a 10G uplink/connection to the backbone as the uplink port(s) are shared by all server ports. Uplinks and backbone connections are nearly always fiber; switch to server connections may be either copper or fiber. Standards based copper ports are usually less expensive and support multiple speeds without a hardware change.

There are standards for cabling and connectivity within a data center. These fall under the direction of TIA, ISO/IEC, Fibre Channel Industry Association, BICSI, and other local standards. Local and international standards generally conform to international standards with additions of local requirements or codes. TIA is predominant in North America, and ISO applies globally, including in North America, although they are often listed together in performance specifications. Standards are *not* codes; however, they provide a least common denominator for communications across their strands and cores, and adherence is highly recommended. The Ethernet Alliance (www.ethernetalliance.org) has provided a roadmap for speeds and media.

LATEST INTERFACES AND NOMENCLATURE

	Backplane	Twinax Cable	Twisted Pair (1 Pair)	Twisted Pair (4 Pair)	MMF	500m PSM4	2km SMF	10km SMF	20km SMF	40km SMF	80km SMF	Electrical Interface
10BASE-	T1S		T1S/T1L									
100BASE-			T1									
1000BASE-			T1	T								
2.5GBASE-	KX		T1	T								
5GBASE-	KR		T1	T								
10GBASE-			T1	T				BIDI Access	BIDI Access	BIDI Access		
25GBASE-	KR	CR/CR-S		T	SR			LR/ EPON/ BIDI Access	EPON/ BIDI Access	ER/ BIDI Access		25GAUI
40GBASE-	KR4	CR4		T	SR4/eSR4	PSM4	FR	LR4				XLAUI XLPPI
50GBASE-	KR	CR			SR		FR	EPON/ BIDI Access LxR	EPON/ BIDI Access	BIDI Access ER		LAUI-2/50GAUI-2 50GAUI-1
100GBASE-	KR4 KR2 KR1	CR10 CR4 CR2 CR1			SR10 SR4 SR2 SR1	PSM4 DR	10X10-2km CWDM4/ FR1 100G-FR	10X10-10km LR4/ 4WDM-10 LR1 100G-LR	4WDM-20	ER4/ 4WDM-40	ZR	CAUI-10 CPPI CAUI-4/100GAUI-4 100GAUI-2 100GAUI-1
200GBASE-	KR4 KR2	CR4 CR2			SR4 SR2	DR4	FR4	LR4		ER4		200GAUI-4 200GAUI-2
400GBASE-	KR4	CR4			SR16 SR8/SR4.2 SR4	DR4	FR8 FR4 400G-FR4	LR8 LR4-6 400G-LR4-10		ER8	ZR	400GAUI-16 400GAUI-8 400GAUI-4

Gray Text = IEEE Standard   Red Text = In Standardization   Green Text = In Study Group
Blue Text = Non-IEEE standard but complies to IEEE electrical interfaces

Figure 36. Ethernet Alliance Roadmap with Interfaces
www.ethernetalliance.org
The number at the end of the interface dictates
the media pairs or strands.
Copper twisted pair uses four pairs.

Channel Terminology

Cabling channels (both copper and fiber) comprise the connectivity attached (patch panel, outlet, plug, terminal blocks, etc.) to the communications media (copper or fiber cable). Some channel specifications are open (they allow mixing of manufacturers within the same category performance), and some are closed to a single manufacturer as the entire channel is tuned for performance. Channels are tuned for additional headroom and margin, which, in layperson's terms, means that the channels operate above the standards.

A note about headroom and margin: all standards are codeveloped with active electronics manufacturers. The standards are minimum performance specifications. For headroom and margin in cable plants, the extra speaks to the manufacturer's quality and may provide some forgiveness factor for poor installations. Headroom and margin will not make your packets move any faster. In fact, *if* the channel is installed correctly and passes testing parameters, a minimally compliant channel will perform as well as one with headroom.

All components for a single standard should be interoperable if the products are component compliant. Of course, occasional non-standard proprietary configurations may be needed for specific applications. The standards are open and do not address proprietary links. Sometimes, a proprietary system's features make it attractive to a project. Examples are special terminations, extended or limiting parameters like distance, varied diameters, conductor size, etc.

From a jack to the patch panel is known as a *permanent link* (see Figure 37 below). Use a permanent link test to test performance. These tests are the most critical for documentation purposes and specifications, as it is likely not to change often. For full *channel* specifications, the patch cords are included at each end of the permanent link to connect the active and test equipment for testing. Some manufacturers automatically include patch cords with a channel warranty if you use their products. It is also important to note that some manufacturers will void your site warranty if you use another manufacturer's patch cords.

When the channel/link connects to a piece of energized equipment, a new channel is tested. Active electronics act to boost the signal before sending it over the channel. In the diagram below, the outside panels would attach to a server on one end and a switch on the other. Each connection degrades the performance a bit, so too many, can render a channel useless.

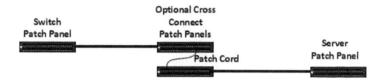

Figure 37. Permanent Link with Optional Cross Connect Adding Patch Cords at the Switch and Server Creates a Channel

Transmissions

As mentioned above, the media for transmission will be either copper or fiber (glass). Copper transmits via electrical pulses, while fiber transmits via light. The higher the speed, the more expensive the port. Typical structured copper media types found in the data center are:

TIA Components	ISO Components/Cabling	Frequency	Highest Speed	Notes
Category 5e	Category 5E/Class D	100MHz	2.5GBASE-T*	Not recommended for data centers, but sometimes used.
Category 6	Category 6/Class E	250MHz	10GBASE-T Max recommended 5GBASE-T	Not recommended for 10G, although there is limited support. It will not support a full 100m channel. Recommended use is only for installed base, not new installations.
Category 6A	Category 6A/Class EA	500 MHz	10GBASE-T	Minimum recommended category of cable for data centers. The cable may be shielded or unshielded. Match termination hardware to the cable construction.
N/A	Category 7/Class F	600MHz	10GBASE-T	No TIA Equivalent
N/A	Category 7A/Class FA	1000MHz	10GBASE-T	No TIA Equivalent,
Category 8	Category 8.1/Class 1 Category 8.2/Class 2	2000MHz	Varies, Data Center ONLY	RJ-45 (8.1) Non-RJ-45 (8.2) Both are Data Center Only for Limited Distance Applications

Any cabling channel consists of the transmission media (copper or fiber) and connectors. ISO/IEC refers to both, while TIA refers to the entire channel. Standards-based connectors allow equipment and components to interface with each other. Generally, standards-based copper channels use RJ45 format outlets and plugs, although Category 7 and 7A use different connectors, TERA and GG-45 specifically.

Likewise, Twinax copper uses a different style of connector. These direct attached copper (DAC) cables may be purchased separately or from active electronics manufacturers. As such, you may be unable to use the cable from one manufacturer with another's equipment. The important thing here is to ensure that your media and connectors will work with your active electronics ports.

Connectors and cabling should be in the same category; if not, the channel is rated as the lowest performing component. So, a category 7 cable with a category 6 connector will be a category 6 channel.

A Quick Word About Testing and Manufacturer Specifications

All manufacturers supply specification sheets for their systems. It is important to note that there is no standard for a test channel. The various combinations of stranded and solid copper and the number of connections will directly impact the test results. For example, a 90m channel with a 5m patch cord at each end will perform differently than the same manufacturer's products with additional connections and different mixes of solid and stranded cords (i.e., 50m solid and two 25m stranded cords). Also, the manufacturer-reported tests come from a lab setting. The exact cable and connectors used may not be the latest shipping iterations. If one is evaluating products, the best solution is to procure enough cable and connectors and do a bake-off with your installer or a consultant. Worst case channels should be 4-connector for testing purposes. Do not compare typical case numbers (averages) to the worst case (worst you can expect from the system). Be sure you are comparing apples to apples.

Shielded versus Unshielded

Along with category, copper cabling has various construction types. The cable's construction may be unshielded twisted pair (UTP), foiled/shielded twisted pair (FTP/STP), or with an overall braided shield around foiled twisted pairs (S/FTP), etc. The cable shield should terminate within the connector attaching to the shielded connector housing. Shielded connectors connect to the grounding bar in a patch panel.

The purpose of the shield is to reject transients (noise) from the channel. The shield terminates at one end of the channel (typically in the data center cross-connect) to the telecommunications main bonding busbar, which connects to the building earth/bond/ground rod. Sharing the ground/earthing/bonding connection eliminates ground loops (where signals loop back via the path of least resistance). It equalizes potential as all transients leave via the single ground. In layperson's terms, we provide the path of least resistance out of the building for any unwanted signals or coupled noise.

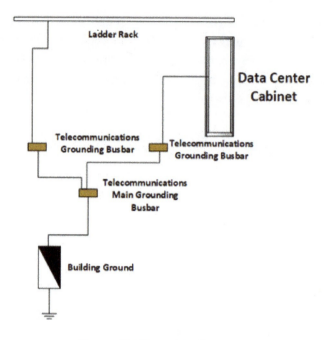

Figure 38. Grounding Diagram

The cable shield also helps with heat dissipation; therefore, the length derating for hot environments using shielded channels is half that of a UTP system channel. The shield can also stop jamming activities and may be a requirement for some governmental installations. Likewise, it is also advantageous in high-noise environments like factories and service corridors. Cable construction is generally preference based. Shielded is a bit more expensive than UTP, but the benefits may be worth the upcharge.

UTP will ignore some noise through its balance but does not have a shield to drain any transient noise, coupled energy, and may be susceptible to jamming.

Figure 39. Examples of Shielded Cables
FTP (Left) and S/FTP (Right)

Patch cords connect the patch panels and the equipment. The patch cord category and shielding should match the channel. Hybrid patch cords are available with different connectors on each end to facilitate connections needing them, but again, the entire channel rates as the lowest performing component. Some data centers use patch cords to connect servers to switches mounted at the top of the same cabinet. In this case, the cable acts as a direct connection, not a channel. Always buy quality patch cords.

Test all copper channels and verify passing results prior to use. Remediate any channels that fail testing. Cable tests will become part of the permanent documentation for the data center. Likewise, they may be needed when troubleshooting electronics to ascertain what is causing the problem. Using untested cabling channels may have mixed results and be a headache when troubleshooting. Noise is intermittent and hard to track.

Copper Systems

Signal losses occur over both copper and fiber. Copper systems are generally designed with less than four connectors. A connector is a faceplate outlet, patch panel, or anywhere two separate segments connect within the channel. Since there is some signal degradation each time you break into a channel, losses within the channels must be managed.

Designs that provide longevity in copper and fiber medium will be the most cost-effective over time. Considerations outside of the media cost include the cost of the electronics, lifetime cost (install, use, rip out, replace), and distances supported.

Overall Cable Plant Considerations

The cladding of copper and fiber must conform to the environment in which it is installed (CODE requirement). Plenum spaces must use plenum cable. Most data centers prefer riser-rated cabling as it is more cost-effective but cannot be installed in a plenum area. Outside the US, LSZH/LS0H Low Smoke Zero Halogen is common and far less expensive than a plenum construction. Since jacketing materials is code restricted, if there is any uncertainly, consult the AHJ.

Low voltage copper cabling can carry power to equipment. While this is not as common in a data center, often PoE (Power over Ethernet) switches that provide work area solutions, power wireless access points, and power security cameras may be in the data center. The best cable for PoE is category 6A shielded. This cable has more copper in the conductors than category 5E or 6 cables. The shield helps dissipate heat.

Fiber Specifics

Fiber uses a variety of connectors based on the number of strands in use and the core. The most common are LC and MTP/MPO (mechanical transfer push-on/ multi-fiber push-on) connectors. Fiber transmissions change the digital signal to light via transceivers at each end of the channel. The transceivers may be part of the interconnect or the active electronics.

FORM FACTORS

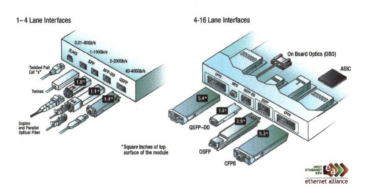

Figure 40. Common Equipment Interfaces for Copper and Fiber Courtesy of the Ethernet Alliance (www.ethernetalliance.org)

Polarity is a means for the transmitter to be paired with a receiver at the opposite end. Think of this like a lane of traffic leaving and another one returning. Going the wrong way leads to collisions or, in the case of fiber, failure. Polarity works through physical fiber or the optics that control the communications. All communications that leave a digital processor must be converted to an optical signal to transmit from one end to the other. The optical to digital conversions may happen internally to the equipment or externally via a transceiver.

The applications, bandwidth, number of strands, and distance will all impact the fiber selection. The number of strands is application dependent. Some applications rely on parallel processing for transmissions. Parallel means several strands transmit packets simultaneously, much like splitting a shipment into multiple trucks, and all trucks travel different lanes down the same highway and all trucks have the same start and destination, and all travel at the same speed.

	Type	Core / Cladding (um)	Fast Ethernet 100Mb	Gigabit GbE	10Gigabit 10GbE	40Gigabit 40GbE	100Gigabit 100GbE	40G SWDM4	100G SWDM4
Multimode	OM1	62.5 / 125	2km	275m	33m	-	-	-	-
	OM2	50 / 125	2km	550m	82m	-	-	-	-
	OM3	50 / 125	2km	800m	300m	100m	100m	240m	75m
	OM4	50 / 125	2km	1100m	400m	150m	150m	350m	100m
	OM5	50 / 125	2km	1100m	400m	150m	150m	440m	150m
Singlemode	OS1/OS2	9 / 125	40km	100km	40km	40km	40km	-	-

Figure 41. Fiber Types, Speeds, and Distances and Colors.

NOTE: OM1 and OM2 are legacy and have been rescinded from the standards. They are included for reference as older installations may still have some.
Higher than 100G is not in the scope of this paper, but the roadmap shows speeds up to 1Tb/s.

Designated OS1 (optical singlemode 1st version) or OS2, singlemode fiber transmission happens via a singlemode (lightwave). Multiple conversations share the fiber via time division or wavelength division multiplexing. Time division can be thought of like the song, "Row, Row, Row Your Boat." Each communication has a different start time. Wavelength division multiplexing uses various wavelengths (colors) to separate the communications conversations.

Multimode fiber (the minimum recommended is OM3 or OM4) uses multiple modes simultaneously, like waves with distinct highs and lows for separation. Each wave of communication has its own space/lane and carries part of the communications packet. Again, carved up by the transmitting end and reassembled by the receiving end.

As with copper, every time we break into a channel to add a connector, we degrade the signal. Too much degradation and the channel is rendered useless. Passive connectors are those within the channel between active electronics components. Therefore, link loss budgets matter. A link loss budget is the total transmission loss allowed in a fiber channel that can be tolerated and still supply the necessary transport of packets. Furthermore, distance attenuates loss.

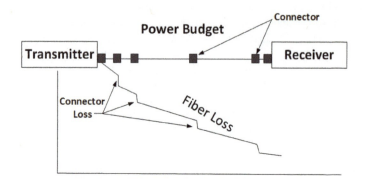

Figure 42. Link losses

Pathways and Spaces

Figure 43. Overhead Pathways

Pathways and spaces refer to the paths cables take from one area to another and the space in which those pathways reside. Pathways and spaces can be inside cabinets, adjacent to racks, underfloor or overhead (see pros and cons of raised floors above). The cable is supported along the way by ladder racks, cable trays, waterfalls (to drop into a cabinet), strain relief, wire management, and other components. Pathways are generally considered full for design purposes at 50% capacity.

Whether under floor or overhead, the idea of pathways is to support the cabling in an organized way properly along the entire channel so performance does not degrade. The twisted pair works because of the twists. Smashing the cable untwists the pairs. Fiber transmits light. Bends keep the light from moving as light doesn't turn corners. Either would create a failure, retransmission, or some other undesirable event.

Pathways are attached to building/room grounding and bonding grids. They must route around building columns, not block hot air egress, must not block air intakes on equipment, and should remain neatly dressed and run following all manufacturer specifications. Manufacturers offer performance warranties on channels. However, if not correctly installed and tested, the warranty is void.

Cable Routing to Equipment

Data center switching/networking equipment can be either centrally located, located within a zone, or distributed to data center cabinets and connected back to a core switch via fiber. Some differences are shown below.

Top of Rack (in Server Rack)	Middle of Row/ End of Row	Zones/Areas
The switch is only for one server rack	Switch supplies networking to a row of cabinets	Switch supplies networking to a few rows or a zone; can save costs on networking equipment in low-density situations
Most cost-effective in higher-density environments	Allows greater utilization of switch ports in lower-density situations	Can be the most cost-effective in low-density environments
No patching area is required; connections to servers via patch cords or jumpers	Requires structured cabling within the row	Required structured cabling within the zone
More switches mean more power connections and fewer rack units for servers	For high-density situations, the patching area may require multiple cabinets	It takes a little more planning as multiple rows are served

Storage and Storage Area Networks (SAN)

Any data we want or need must reside on some type of storage device. Server storage disks can be as simple as an internal hard drive or more complex storage arrays. Some servers have internal hard drives to boot up but utilize storage arrays for application data. Storage arrays can include hard drives installed in disparate servers pooled together via software. Network-attached storage (NAS) and SAN arrays and towers are standalone storage devices.

Storage arrays communicate with servers through SAN directors. These operate much like a switch assuring access to servers and backup sources alike. Standard storage protocols include TCP/IP over Ethernet, Fibre Channel, Infiniband, and SCSI (internal). These devices predominantly connect via fiber. The number of strands of fiber depends on the application and the speed. In a few cases, devices use standards-based copper channels or direct attached copper cables. Beware because as you design these, link loss budgets (see fiber section) are not the same across all protocol stacks or distances.

In most cases, files are written to storage in such a way that if one drive fails, the information is recreated from information on other drives. This level of redundancy is known as RAID (Redundant Array of Integrated/Inexpensive Disks). The "I" in the acronym has dual meanings depending on the manufacturer, but the process is the same. Different levels of RAID exist, each defined by the number of drives and how the data writes to each drive.

For backup purposes, sometimes, drive writes are mirrored to additional internal drives in real time. In other cases, files are simultaneously written to multiple arrays. The server writes to a storage array that then, via a separate connection, duplicates that information to another array for high-availability, real-time backup. And in other cases, the data is backed up to the cloud. Other centers use optical or tape to back up information and take it off-site. Drives may be mechanical disks called hard disk drives (HDD) or solid-state drives (SSD) without the mechanical moving parts. SSDs are rapidly overtaking the market. Optical disks are often used for backups.

Data Center Cabling Examples

High availability networking consists of dual switches supporting primary and secondary network connections in servers and storage equipment. The copper or fiber carry packets to the networking switch. Switches can be located within the same cabinet as the server (Top of Rack), at the end of a row, or more centrally located.

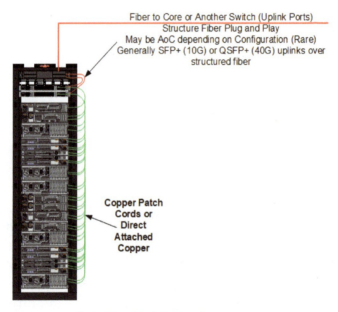

Typical Top of Rack Configuration
Inside a Cabinet – Generally Two Network Connections to Each Server
Generally Co-exists with structured cabling for management and monitoring
Network DAC Cu shown for Connectivity

Figure 44. Top of Rack

There is less traffic leaving the rack than servers in the cabinet (the servers don't always talk and certainly don't communicate full time simultaneously). Assuming that not all network cards will be active at once is called oversubscription. Twenty servers, each with gigabit network cards, do not consistently produce twenty gigs of traffic. In reality, there may only be a few servers using the network simultaneously. Servers perform many duties internally that involve zero network communications. Some applications are more input-output (I/O) intensive and rely more on high throughput networks.

A bottleneck occurs when the network can't keep up with traffic at any point. The concept is very similar to a toll booth or busy freeway exit. Traffic slows down through the choke point. Servers may talk locally to a network switch or storage switch. When that traffic must move to another switch to get to another part of the network, the Internet, or outside the data center, it does so via the uplink ports (often fiber) that make up the network's backbone (core) connecting all the switches.

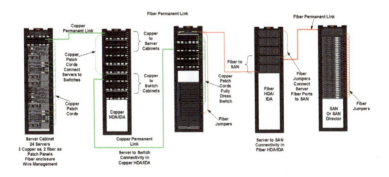

Figure 45. Logical Example of Copper and Fiber Layouts. Full Structured Cabling

Some or all the above channels may be used. In some cases, SAN directors and switches are also located in the cabinet with the server, in some cases they are at the end of a row or centrally located. Working with the storage, networking, and server teams will help design the best solutions.

In some hyperscale environments roll in a fully loaded cabinet with servers and switches that connect to overhead or underfloor systems. If there is a failure in the cabinet, a new cabinet replaces it and the units are triaged later.

Overall View

Perhaps the easiest way to understand the connectivity is to look at logical layouts across a larger data center. Shown in the following three examples is a top view of one quadrant of a larger data center installation. The cabinets at the far right are actually in the middle of the facility, but only one quarter is being shown for clarity.

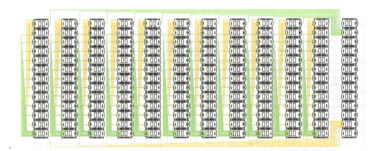

Figure 46. Sample Overall Fiber Connectivity Design
(Top View)

Centralized components (core networking and SAN director connections) are at the right end. End of row switches and SAN switch components are connected to the core vial the green (primary) and yellow (secondary) fiber uplinks. Each server cabinet within the row connects to the switches at the end of the row. This design utilizes fiber throughout. Management switches are in each server rack and also connected via the fiber uplinks.

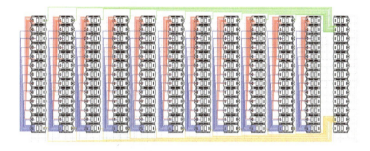

Figure 47. Logical Connectivity Copper and Fiber End of Row (Top View)

In the above example, primary copper (blue) and secondary copper (red) connect to switches at the end of the row. Copper remains in row. Those switches connect to the core and WAN at the right via fiber uplinks.

Which of the above methods is used depends on several factors. In general, it is wise to do a cost analysis of cabling, switch costs, power to operate the switches, and ongoing maintenance costs which renew annually. In some instances, it is significantly less to use more cabling and fewer switches. In others, especially higher density configurations, top of rack is preferred. For low density situations, the switches can be mounted above cabinets to be shared by the servers in adjacent cabinets. It's a numbers game, for sure. Sometimes the design for one equipment iteration is very different from the next.

It pays to do your costing and operations exercises and not just go with the latest trend.

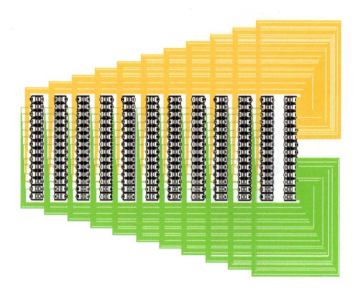

Figure 48. Logical Connectivity - Centralized Patching

In the last example, one can see how complex a centralized switch can be. That said, in some cases it is less expensive to operate a centralized switching and SAN environment, even taking into account the additional cable quantities and lengths. Pathway fill is an important consideration.

Wide Area Equipment – Entrance Facilities

There will also be an area of the data center for the wide-area equipment (routers), firewalls, and security appliances. Centers will generally have primary and secondary networks and sometimes out-of-band management. When communications need to leave the center for the outside world, it does so via the WAN (Wide Area Networking) area.

Telecommunications equipment belonging to any carriers occupies this area. The carrier demarcation may need to be extended into this space. Some facilities will have this equipment in a separate, secured room called a meet-me room (colocation facilities). The meet-me room is an area where the carriers come into the building, and there is a cross-connect allowing occupants to connect to the telecommunications carriers.

Equipment in this area will occupy a few racks. This equipment may be at the entrance facility/room or on the data center floor via extended demarcation. In corporate facilities, the voice switch/PBX may also be in this area.

Routers are intelligent switch like devices that understand enough information from each packet to decide if that traffic is internal or external to the data center.

Firewalls act as traffic cops for the facility. A firewall allows or blocks traffic in and out of the facility based on any number of rules. Firewalls keep bad actors out and inside people from engaging with bad external sites. Firewalls also act as a proxy to mask internal addresses, so they are not visible to the outside world. The concept is like a fake email account that forwards to your own, thereby concealing your email address.

DMZs (demilitarized zones) are networks in between the public network (outside) and the internal network (LAN). For instance, if a company has a public website, the server needs a public (can be seen by the outside) address. Internal addresses should remain invisible to the Internet.

APPLICATIONS AND OPERATIONS

Cybersecurity

Figure 49

Part of the DMZ equipment above doubles as part of any entity's cybersecurity strategy. Cybersecurity refers to the non-physical security of the environment. All systems should be included. Cybersecurity keeps bad actors out, secures corporate data assets, limits system visibility, stops disruption of services, fends off ransomware, etc. Whether an entity operates its own facility or operates in another's, all assets fall under the cyber umbrella of protection.

Zero trust is a term that refers to trust levels assigned to any user. The premise is that the network and applications trust no one. Users are granted permission only for the resources they need to function in their job. With cyber threats today, total lockdown is prudent.

SASE (Secure Access Secure Edge) and SD-WAN (Software-Defined WAN) allow access to a network after a user has authenticated and not before. Resources visible to the user are the only resources the user can access. These edge-level access control mechanisms deny by default and set up secure access.

VPN (Virtual Private Network) is the act of creating a wide area network connection that mimics being on the local area network (LAN). Communications occur via a secure tunnel through the insecure Internet. Think of a VPN has your own personal lane of traffic on a public highway. Your car is the encapsulation that shields it from all other cars like a cloak of invisibility.

Some components of cybersecurity include:

- Access and access controls
- Permissions
- Passwords
- Threat detection and remediation
- Application security
- Cloud security
- Storage and data security in transit and at rest (encryption)
- Change management
- Retention policies
- Proprietary and personally identifiable information protection
- End-user education
- Penetration testing

Where different sites interconnect, secure tunnels or communications channels are necessary. Cyber responsibilities cover any threat to data from internal or external sources. Cyber security professionals must constantly update plans and resources to guard against new threats. Furthermore, DR plans must address what happens when security components are down. For instance, what if the firewall goes down? Cybersecurity is another highly specialized field.

Physical and cybersecurity teams use **security incident and event management (SIEM)** software. SIEM systems can be as complex as needed for the organization. The sale, administration, and training for this software help companies use the features to their fullest extent. This software can provide historical data used for insights into future solutions.

Monitoring and Sensors

When the data center is under construction, this is the best time to install monitoring for environmentals, power, leak detection, lighting sensors to support lights out, and any other necessary tracking. Capacity planning relies on either brain power alone (spreadsheets) or actual intelligence derived from installed sensors. The sensors may be small, but their information is instrumental to many operations.

Other sensors like motion detection can trigger alarms or cameras to ascertain what personnel are doing within the space as part of the overall security strategy.

Cloud

Figure 50

People use the term the cloud. It makes it seem as if there is only one cloud. But, in reality, there are many. For the sake of this book, the cloud is a data center. A cloud has ready to use resources that can be spun up or consumed in an instant as opposed to weeks. Cloud tenants rent assets or consume hardware and software maintained by others. There are many applications, certifications, and specialties in the cloud alone. It is an exciting field!

To understand the cloud, it helps to know some background. Suppose a company is a large retailer. That retailer builds out its entire data center infrastructure, including the space, machines, power, cooling, and infrastructure to support the Christmas rush. What happens to all those assets and contracts for the remaining part of the year? They incur costs. Telecommunications contracts are not month to month, neither are power commitments, space commitments, etc. Suppose that company could rent out currently used capacity to others during down periods. Instead of all that infrastructure being a drain on the bottom line, it enhances the bottom line. This is a great example of cloud – computing using others resources. The above is not the only scenario, as providers now build out cloud resources just for that revenue. Seasonal, promotional, and fixed period campaigns and traffic can happen in another provider's cloud and return the resources to the provider at the end. Sports teams and racing are examples of seasonal cloud consumers.

A company can be fully in the cloud using public cloud resources only. They can operate in a hybrid fashion with some on-premises and some assets in the public cloud. Or they can build out their own private cloud. Multi-cloud environments refer to companies utilizing multiple cloud providers. While these can provide significant cost benefit, it also adds to complexity. Using multiple providers can also ensure that at least some systems are operational if the other clouds become inaccessible.

Due to the vastness of cloud topics, we will not dwell on it here but know that the cloud and its applications are just interconnected data centers. Providers build facilities for high availability, meaning designs include high redundancy *and* high resiliency. Every job that is available in the data center industry is available in the cloud.

Consumers use public cloud services for a variety of reasons. Still, most hinge on a company saving the costs of building a data center (or some part), maintaining it, and keeping the personnel on the payroll for these tasks.

Cloud consumers may choose from any or all of the below:

Infrastructure as a Service (IaaS) allows consumers to procure infrastructure (servers, networking, and storage) via the cloud. Rightsizing is paramount, as oversizing will lead to overspending. Under sizing will lead to a need to upgrade in the future, but as the cloud is elastic, adding is easy. Not all cloud applications port from one cloud to another. IaaS provides the greatest control of all cloud models. It is most like running your data center in someone else's facility.

Platform as a Service (PaaS) allows consumers to rent platforms for application development. It keeps users from needing to know about the hardware piece. Security is still the responsibility of the consumer. Users do not need to know and administer the hardware to develop via the platform.

Software as a Service (SaaS) is probably the most common. Users consume software from the cloud. The data generally resides in the cloud with the application provider, although some hybrid environments also utilize local copies. Gmail® and Salesforce® are examples. This model is prevalent across all types of end-users. While companies may not use it for everything, they will undoubtedly use it for some applications. Cybersecurity is a good example.

Serverless is like PaaS in that the backend equipment remains hidden from the end user. The most significant difference is that serverless is a native cloud (designed to live in the cloud) platform, and as such, it scales without user intervention. Users pay on a per-use basis.

Here are a couple of points to note about the cloud:

- Cloud costs can fluctuate greatly! Companies need to understand costs.
- Egress fees can be massive. It is expensive to get data out of the cloud and move it around in the cloud. Understand all the charges upfront.
- Not all cloud platforms port (move) to other cloud platforms.

- Know what you are doing! Incorrectly setting up permissions and security is a guaranteed headache down the road.

Be sure to right size cloud operations and regularly monitor costs. Finally, a *critical* point to understand is that while the provider's cloud environment is secure, the consumer/end-user is 100% responsible for their security configuration within the cloud. According to industry experts, most cloud misconfigurations go unnoticed until exploitation occurs.

Data Sovereignty

Data sovereignty is becoming an increasingly prominent concern. It works hand in hand with privacy laws, but the idea is to govern where data personally identifiable information (PII) data is stored. Data should be encrypted both at rest and in transit. But *where* that data is stored is often mandated by law. When spinning up cloud instances, pay particular attention should there be a need for PII. There is an extra fee to select specific locations with some cloud providers. Plan up front for the best solution.

Operations and Management

While it may seem that we have spent a lot of time on the building, bits, and parts, any of the above topics, as part of the ecosystem, need regular maintenance and management. New projects need sourcing. IT employees evaluate solutions, maintain capacity plans, develop applications, administer security, manage cloud resources, clean, handle IP addressing, etc.

Positions may be remote, in-house, or outsourced (provided by others). Consultants can fill in for projects when internal resources are time strapped. In the jobs listing below, just know that there is a plentiful number of employers for any of them.

Operations personnel get involved in lots of forward-thinking projects. These can include new equipment selection, customer requirements, evaluations, procurement, and all sorts of things! But of course, it depends on the job requirements and management needs regarding individual projects.

Disaster Recovery and Business Continuity

Outages are inevitable. How a company recuperates is critical to its ability to stay in business. First and foremost, defining the difference between disaster recovery and business continuity planning is pertinent. Disaster recovery is just that: recovering after a disaster. Business continuity planning refers to a business operating during and after a disaster. In short, it means keeping the business running continuously. Responses will vary depending on the severity of the disaster.

First and foremost is to *have* a plan. The plan will be a work in progress as business processes change. Revision control is vital! Backup copies of the plan should be stored off-site or at least be electronically accessible, with one hard copy on-site and another in a safe, accessible location. Remember that disasters don't always happen from 8 a.m. to 5 p.m., so a bank vault might not be the best location for many of these documents. Likewise, online locations may not be accessable.

Each plan should have several sections, the first being contact information for the BC/DR team (from now on, called the DR team). The team should consist of representation from every department, not just IT. In particular, facilities, security, safety, computer operations, CIO/IT management, HR, finance, executive, production, engineering, manufacturing, customer services, sales, vendor representatives, reception, technical support, data entry, landlord contacts, etc. There should be a formal notification chain, including the C-Suite, security, the DR team, courier services, customer notifications, account numbers, and all vendor support contacts. The DR/BC team should meet quarterly (more often during large projects) to review any changes to the plan and coordinate revisions amongst the team. Don't assume that anything won't matter. Bring any and all changes up at team meetings. Even a tiny change in one application can have an impact on another.

The second section should include site information as applicable. This section will consist of backup site locations, locations for software copies, checks, hosting information, as well as contact and access information for every site dependent on this site. Longer-term disasters will require the establishment of a command-and-control center. The plans and resources to do so should be included as well.

The environment documentation section includes data center diagrams and documentation. You can't fix it if you can't find it. This documentation should consist of all active circuit identification numbers, IP addresses, and contact numbers for carriers. In addition, all hardware, software, addresses, and revision/patch information, as well as asset location information, is contained in this section. It is prudent to have both logical and physical layout diagrams.

Each team member that has control of an asset should be listed. Asset interconnections and dependencies reside in this section of the plan. It is also helpful if these diagrams contain risk factor numbers or some readily identifiable ranking and/or color to indicate what needs to come back up first. Remember the KISS principle: Keep It Simple, Silly.

The following section can create volumes when done correctly. This section includes processes and procedures. As employees document the tasks and details for their job, it's a good idea to have that person swap with someone who knows nothing about their job. The person holding the documentation should do the original person's job by the documented procedures alone.

Swapping accomplishes two things. First, it's an excellent exercise for cross-training. Second, it allows the documentation to include the one-off things the primary documenter may have missed; think, "You can just ignore that message." Documentation should be maintained and updated with every patch, revision, or change in applications/hardware.

Ideally, "Readiness to Respond" documentation gets tested *before* disaster strikes. Train, test, remediate, test again, then test regularly. Unfortunately, the press is full of examples of no or DR plans gone wrong. Outages and errors become public quickly!

Quality Assurance and Root Cause Analysis

These specialties operate across the data center industry and its companies. Quality processes follow formalized guidelines, which allow manufacturing and processes to be improved constantly.

Root cause analysis (RCA) is the process of forensically investigating problems, outages, and downtime to assure the causes are addressed in the continuous improvement cycle. RCA involves anyone with involvement in the procedure under inspection. These exercises are not designed to be punitive. Personnel matters are outside of this exercise. Rather, these exercises work to find the actual cause, which could be procedural, training, malfunction, or something else. Fish diagrams are often used to help map the process.

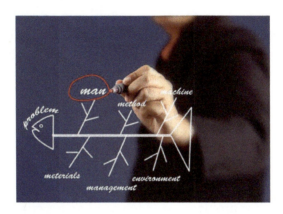

Figure 51. Fish Diagram Example to Outline Inputs

RCA Steps include:

1. Determine the problem
2. Gather information from all stakeholders
3. Determine the root cause
4. Find corrective or preventative actions
5. Draft the corrective actions and train personnel
6. Monitor and measure to assure the solution has the intended benefits
7. Lather, rinse, and repeat as needed
8. Document the final outcomes and publish to the team

Project Management

Project managers are employed across the industry. These individuals are there to assure that project personnel are on task, have what they need, logistics are sorted, tasks are defined, and all things happen according to timelines set at the project kick-off. Often, project managers run multiple projects at one time. Project management is one area from building to coding that follows the same rules. The tasks may vary, but the project management methodology applies to them all.

There are two main theories behind project management: waterfall and Agile, also known as SCRUM. Waterfall works over the entire project, milestones, and dependencies, while Agile breaks projects into small sections of tasks to obtain a minimal viable product. Quick daily standup meetings identify hurdles and actions taken and forthcoming to keep the team on track and assure that problems are identified and rectified early. Certifications are available for both.

Coding and Database Management

Coding gets a lot of attention. Writing computer programs is a bit like a brain teaser and can be fun. There are massive resources and groups for webmasters, web administrators, digital marketers, coders, database administrators, cloud architects, user experience professionals, project managers (Agile and waterfall), artificial intelligence and big data mining, blockchain and bitcoin miners, and the like. We will not go into detail here due to the wealth of information and curricula supporting these; just know that there are mission-critical jobs for all of these and more.

Database managers and administrators work to ensure that the data sets a company uses are maintained and that the relationships between them are secure. Admins keep up with record retention, data structures, and how the data should be used.

Remote hands is a concept where the colocation provider has "intelligent" hands at the other end of a phone to assist companies with a variety of issues when their staff is unavailable or not on-site, or the company uses remote hands exclusively.

Help desk personnel are also in high demand. These folks take and track calls for desktop, server, security, or other device support. Help desk services may or may not tie with an NOC, depending on a company's organizational structure. The help desk is just as important in a data center as it is to the user community, if not more so.

Bitcoin and blockchain companies also use data centers for processing and mining. However, as the code is structured differently, the facilities may or may not have the redundancy of other data centers. They generally do not have standby power resources as the code, by design, operates across multiple sites simultaneously. Bitcoin facilities look different than a regular data center due to the miners and many draw significantly more power that a traditional facility. (below).

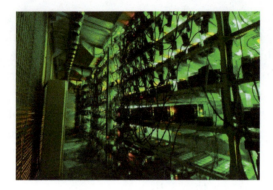

Figure 52. Bitcoin miners

Cloud professionals work with applications and databases as well. Don't forget to check out the various certifications for clouds, containers (cloud native programs), big data, AI, architects and other topics.

DevOps refers to the development of software and the operations of that software. These folks develop applications and database schemas, customize software applications for business use, sometimes test hardware, and set up resiliency and failover practices for software owned and used by the company.

SecOPS is the practice of wrapping security around all operations with a security-first mindset (see the cybersecurity section).

Procurement

Procurement is mentioned, as this can be a highly specialized area. It is difficult to become a consumer of products you know nothing about without some help. Buying the first solution, what your buddy bought, or the first one from a web search may or may not be a good idea.

As the data center is an ecosystem, products must work in that environment without disrupting other solutions. Administrators, technicians, and vendors can all help. Still, it is imperative to understand spheres of influence, personal gains, short-term and long-term goals, interoperability, and a wide range of parameters as you take in any advice.

Vendor management is daunting at large corporations. In fact, sometimes, departments are forced to work with vendors that may or may not be the best simply because it is too much trouble to add a new vendor or remove an old one. Therefore, it's a great idea that procurement, vendor management, and the stakeholders work together from the concept through post-purchase follow-up. If you work for a vendor and are selling into the industry, take some time to get to know the procurement folks.

Requests for Information (RFI) is a formal document asking vendors for information to help companies evaluate solutions. These documents are based on a statement of need. For example,

> *Company A wishes to procure a CRM system that supports XX number of employees located in XX locations. Components of the system should include: (insert list here).*

It's always a good idea to ask for cost-saving alternatives, additional feature options not listed, and anything else of interest in this fishing expedition. Then, when you narrow down the results, you can invite them for demonstrations, purchase demo versions or test components, etc. Opening up the net brings knowledge transfer and product knowledge, and teams may find exceptional solutions previously unknown. The process does, however, take time. As such it should be used for long term systems (think accounting) and where enough knowledge to make an informed decision is lacking. Smaller systems are easy to change, foundational systems are much more difficult to replace. It's important to note that not all vendors have an appetite for responding to RFIs, so use them sparingly and when necessary.

RFQ/RFP (request for quote/request for proposal) are terms often used interchangeably. There are pros and cons to the quoting process. From a company perspective, this is a great way to get vendors in your format answering your questions so that you can formulate a decision. Some of these bids are very intricate. Some companies use these to get to the lowest cost bidder (not always a good idea), while others use them as standard procedures to find value, features, ROI, etc. For smaller users, it may be challenging to get enough responses as not all companies wish to spend the time answering.

Often companies have a purchasing threshold that requires an RFP over a certain dollar amount. RFP/RFQ documents can answer many questions, from interoperability to escalation procedures. With or without the RFI step, both can accelerate knowledge of various products and features. This advanced understanding is good for the company and invaluable personal knowledge.

Some companies' sole source for the benefits a single supplier brings to their organization, like training, service advantages, fewer parts, fewer vendors to deal with, or any number of reasons. Some companies are the opposite and require bids for all or most projects.

There will be times when procurement decisions don't allow time for RFI/RFP/RFQ cycles. Sometimes, it is simply too much work for the effort at hand. Some companies are too small and don't have the bandwidth or resources to commit. In these instances, it is wise to look for **brokers and subagents**. These solution providers pick up the tab for commissions, so there is no cost to you. Subagents can provide the short version of features and products. They help select products that will move you forward based on your budget and needs. As brokers work with multiple providers, they are vendor agnostic.

Brokers and subagents work with telecommunications lines, data center spaces, applications, cloud services, disaster recovery packages, data center space, phone systems, unified communications, contact centers, cybersecurity, and a myriad of other software and services. Subagents can provide a great shortcut to your research.

RESOURCES AND SCHOLARSHIPS

Trade Associations

There are several helpful trade associations with expanded literature on all of these topics. The organizations often are little to no cost for students, first-time attendees, and end-users. Several provide local and regional education, virtual, in-person, or hybrid trade shows, and networking opportunities. If you are interested in finding a career (which, if you are reading this, I'm assuming you are), these are great places to meet and greet. See the resources section at the end for some of the most established associations and trade groups.

The Need for Trades, Women, and Vets in Tech – Solving the Critical Talent Shortage

It is difficult to pick up any data center publication without reading about a critical data center skills shortage (translated opportunities). The problem crosses all cities, countries, and anywhere data exists. In short, it is ubiquitous. Even as large tech companies lay off employees, those laid off get scooped up by others in short order. The shortage is not just for IT staff, either. These shortages are greatly evident in the supporting trades. Building diversity in this talent vacuum is not easy.

In some cases, talent problems are self-induced. That is to say, companies are not always effective at looking outside the proverbial box at potential solutions. Patient, heal thyself. Larger tech cities/communities, by and large, attract tech talent leaving voids in other geographies.

Resource deserts are growing as colocation hubs expand. These hub cities also tend to have data center curricula due to the growing need for personnel resources and work with local programs. But by and large, just the knowledge of the data center industry and the jobs within it remain an enigma to most up-and-coming potentials to the talent pool. However, there are undoubtedly efforts to change that through education and exposure at younger ages.

Trades

The trades, in general, have suffered over the years. Society and parents have drilled the need for a degree into our children from a young age. But let there be no mistake that *without the trades, there are no data centers. We owe the trades everything; without them, nothing would be built!*

People remain non-degreed for a variety of reason. Not all people want to proceed down a degree path for various reasons. Skill-gifted people prefer to work with their hands and may seek apprenticeship programs. Not all would-be scholars have the financial resources or time due to other obligations. Not all degree offerings exist in convenient locations. Roughly 80 percent of students start down a degree path only to later change their major, which may lead to a continuity break in their college experience. Some people are not good at taking tests.

We need to encourage people to be happier in their careers, degree or not. In fact, the trades are not only in demand, but there are also **critical shortages** across trade occupations. For example, with the current level of scarcity for electricians, new electricians are poised to begin earning six figures with *zero* college debt. Currently, electricians' median pay in the US is around $75,000, again, without college debt.

Training for skilled-trade jobs often involves apprenticeship programs and little, if any, college. However, junior colleges and other two-year institutions offer training. Programs are available for construction, low voltage, security, plumbing, facilities, and a plethora of other related and in demand trades. The introduction of the data center industry to skilled trades is just as crucial as an introduction to STEM (science, technology, engineering, and math) fields.

Some trades take advantage of the industry opportunities to grow into other positions through certifications and OJT.

Degrees and Non-degreed Professionals

Regarding degrees, many jobs in this industry do not require four-year or even advanced degrees. Degrees have their place and are sometimes mandatory. However, degrees don't necessarily equip a person to take off running in a job. The correlation of the degree requirements doesn't necessarily jibe with the job skills required. The imbalance between curriculum and the rapid advancement of technology has received a sizable amount of press of late.

With rapidly changing technology and a slow-moving curriculum after graduating, OJT or certification courses are often needed to fill the knowledge gaps. Think of it this way: very few people in this industry have degrees in data centers. Furthermore, most degrees with data center majors are brand new outside of architecture and engineering. Even for engineers, data center design is generally a project not a class.

For some people, the lure of paid education is a great incentive to join a company before finishing their degree. Paid tuition is a great perk and a good way for a company to show an interest in employee growth. Working on the job helps to direct one to the desired degree path. Students who graduate with significant student debt tend to job hop into higher-paid positions, often leaving employers to earn more in an effort to pay down debt. Offering paid tuition is not much of a benefit if a company only hires those who wouldn't need the reimbursement. But it is a great benefit to anyone wanting to further their knowledge.

Diversity and Women in Tech

Minorities bring diversity in thought to the workforce. While the conversation about diversity tends to get media attention around minorities, the topic of diversity within the industry is vast. Young, old, rich, not yet rich, western/eastern, college trained/self-taught are all examples. Women, likewise, bring diversity in thought processes.

Diversity also is introduced via those with alternate education methods. In 2021, according to the US Census Bureau's current survey, 37.9 percent of the US population (including retirees and those who have exited the workforce) held at least a four-year degree, including 14 percent who hold advanced degrees. These low numbers indicate the majority of potential workers, both male and female, are without college degrees.

Women make up only 20 percent of engineering graduates, and an even smaller number (11 percent) of practicing engineers are women. In the mid-1980s, 37 percent of computer science majors were women, but in 2019 that dropped to 18 percent, according to dreamhost.com, *State of Women in Tech* scratch (found here).

Moreover, women hold only 25 percent of computing jobs. Nevertheless, the demand for women is increasing! Women are historically not trained to toot our own horns. It is a process we must learn. Many remarkable women in this industry give their time to mentor, sponsor, and uplift other women. Seek them out. Look at the organizations that have women's chapters. Many do. Find women to network with and keep close. Your network is everything. Look for companies with women on their boards of directors. Study after study has proven that companies that embrace diversity and include women on their boards are more profitable than those that don't.

Veterans, Spouses, and Their Children

Veterans are welcome and a highly sought-after group in this industry. Organizations provide training for vets returning to civilian life to equip them with data center skills. Operations, project management, construction, leadership, adaptability to new situations, quick-thinking, confidentiality, and organizational skills directly map to data center positions. In fact, some organizations seek out military spouses and children of vets for much the same reasons; many offer free and on-the-job training.

There are many hard skills from the military that directly translate to the data center space. Indeed, anything cyber or IT is applicable. But many military units are masters at construction, repairs, infrastructure, security, and other jobs that directly transfer.

There have been efforts within the industry to reach out to transition assistance programs (TAPs) within the military, but TAP officers may not understand the vastness of the opportunities. Scholarships are also available. The accompanying podcast series has several interviews with veterans who have joined the industry who can provide insights into their transitions and jobs.

The US Chamber of Commerce has a section for transitioning service members and their spouses. The spouse program pays six weeks of an person's pay and the transitioning service member receives twelve weeks of pay from the government.

Scholarships and Resources

There are many scholarships in this industry that, year after year, go unclaimed. The resources section lists some of these. Often, companies reimburse tuition. Some offer monetary assistance while you are getting a degree. In addition, manufacturers provide training discounts for users. For non-users, follow the manufacturer for specials, and don't feel that you have to be a user to take their training classes. Additional resources and any updates can be found via our Linkedin® group and through the associations and organizations listed below. A portion of the proceeds from this book will help fund scholarships through some of these organizations.

- MikeRoweWorks is an organization that works to help those in the skilled trades.
- iMasons (www.imasons.org) – The infrastructure Masons is an organization of "Builders of the Digital Age." Their motto is Connect, Grow, Give Back. They also have a podcast called the Digital Foundation Podcast, which discusses various industry topics with industry experts. They also have a scholarhip program for those wishing to enter the industry.

- 7x24Exchange – I love this organization as they have one of the most cohesive Women in Mission Critical (WIMCO) and were one of the first to do so. They have national and local chapter events, including local WIMCO events with a plethora of content. Some have scholarships as well, but in all cases these chapters and the national chapter provide exceptional content. They are also the founding organization behind International Data Center Day. Watch for the festivities.
- The Nomad Futurist Foundation is a 501(c)(3) non-profit organization established to demystify the world of digital infrastructure and the related technologies that impact every aspect of our daily lives. Our primary focus is to empower and inspire younger generations through exposure to the underlying technologies that power our digital world and cultivate the next generation of industry leaders. Through the contributions of supporters, they are launching global programs in partnership with a range of education providers, NGOs and other nonprofit organizations committed to educating children in underprivileged communities, promoting diversity and inclusion, and opening up opportunities for growth and new career paths.
- AFCOM – Another excellent organization that has local chapter events and national events. Data Center World is their national event, and it provides impressive educational content and some scholarships.
- AITP – American Institute of Technology Professionals offers information technology education.

- ASIS – A security organization that has standards, local chapters, education, and certifications. Although they don't have a data center industry focus, their certifications still apply. They do have scholarships in the security industry.
- BICSI – has its shows and multiple certification classes. In addition, they have their own data center and project management standards. Although this started as predominantly fiber and low voltage, they have branded and included data center design. BICSI also has national events twice a year and regional chapter events good for networking and knowledge.
- CompTIA – Computer Technology Industry Associations has a large membership and offers technology training and certifications.
- Dice/Bisnow are conferences around the US with great educational content and also a place to learn about job opportunities.
- IEEE – The key standards organization for many of the standards in information technology and electronics today. IEEE welcomes participation from all members. The IEEE Standards Association allows those not traveling to the meetings to participate in the standards process. These standards, while voluntary, assure interoperability.
- Ethernet Alliance – All things Ethernet, standards assistance, forecasts, and interoperability information.
- ASHRAE – Standards for data center rooms, airflow, humidity, and temp.
- CENELEC – The European Electrotechnical Committee for Standardization is one of three European Standardization Organizations

(together with CEN and ETSI) recognized by the European Union and European Free Trade Association (EFTA) for developing and defining voluntary standards at European level.
- SNIA – Storage Networking Industry Association has standards and information for the storage world.
- Infiniband Trade Association sets the standards for communications and media over Infiniband protocols.
- PMI and SCRUM Alliance are two disparate methodologies for project management. PMI has its own certification. Likewise, there are multiple SCRUM certification bodies.
- ISO/IEC is an international standards body that interfaces with IEEE on some projects but operates its practice. As a result, there are multiple ISO certifications that companies seek. These certifications cover business practices, electrical performance, and a lot of others.
- TIA/EIA/ANSI is predominantly North American standard body, but is also referenced and used in some other countries.
- OIF – Optical Industry Foundation has a wealth of information on fiber applications and interoperability.
- FOA – Fiber Optic Association; additional fiber resource
- The Green Grid is a consortium of vendors and consumers dedicated to environmental and sustainability efforts in data center environments.
- The Open Compute Project is not covered in this book, but open compute is another set of standards driven largely by hyperscalers. The

goal is to provide the most energy efficient, repeatable compute stacks. They opening share their work and designs.
- *Data Center Knowledge* is a newsletter that will keep you abreast of industry happenings.
- *DataCenter Frontier* is another popular vendor-agnostic publication resource. Their industry blogs and publications track current events and technology within the data center industry.
- *Network Computing* offers a variety of training and webinars on a variety of topics.
- *Inside Networks* is another insightful industry publication.
- *Mission Critical Magazine* is another publication dedicated to the data center industry.
- Women's Tech Forum is a group of industry women and a great place to network.
- Women Leading Technology Sorority – scholarships and networking for STEAM careers.
- Manufacturers' users' groups and forums provide great information, certifications, and education. Sometimes they are free or heavily discounted for end users. But as a side note, they won't offer competitor information. Challenge the information as it relates to your situation and environment. If you want to pursue an industry-specific certification to further your career, pick one that lots of companies use.
- Government resources are generally public (save any secret info). In the US, www.grants.gov, although tedious, can be a potential funding arm. One can find resources on energy, security, building, etc. Remember, the governments have their own data centers, too.

- Last Mile Education Fund was started to help with grants for side expenses when getting a degree. Services include grants to get you to an interview, pay rent if it will keep someone from dropping out of school, get a car repaired, and a variety of other assistance.
- Aspire2STEAM.org provides scholarships and mentoring for girls entering STEAM professions. Scholarships fund certifications and college.
- Salute Mission Critical – are involved globally throughout the industry bringing veterans into mission critical. They have resources for training and recruitment. They hire and operate with veterans in and from several countries.
- Overwatch is a services organization run and staffed with many military members turned civilian. The US Chamber of Commerce and US Chamber Foundation both have programs for military personnel re-entering civilian life and their spouses. These programs provide paid internships for military families.
- DCAC is the Data Center Anti Conference and a panel styled information format covering a variety of industry topics.
- Various construction and trade associations (there are many).

Certification Resources

Certifications are a great way to learn new things and show that you have a command of that knowledge. Therefore, these certifications are highly sought after. Many are an immersion process, while some require large amounts of time. Certifications are not generally a four-year process like a degree. Some of the above scholarships are also available for certifications, but not all are, so check.

In addition to the associations above, some other industry certification resources are:

- CNet Training has an extensive list of industry certifications from design to operations. They also have a master's degree through their partnership with Anglia Ruskin.
- EPI has a roadmap and training like the above but does not have collegiate-level classes.
- IDCA offers a similar roadmap but also provides a rapid immersion certification path.
- Manufacturers offer many certification programs.
- The major cloud platforms offer cloud certifications.
- Industry Associations (listed elsewhere) offer certifications that are vendor agnostic.
- Unions and apprenticeship programs.
- Other online training resources.

The above is not an inclusive list.

Specialty application certifications exist everywhere. Check some out!

MOOCs

Massive open online courses (MOOCs) are college classes available to audit at little to no charge. These are the same classes taught in college but without the tuition, tests, and grades. These are an often- overlooked resource for a wealth of knowledge available on your schedule to complete the classes. You will not receive college credit, just the knowledge and a happy boost to your resume.

Podcasts

Figure 53

For some great insights into jobs, resources available, companies in the industry, veteran guidance, etc., tune into the accompanying podcast series, "Careers for Women, Trades, and Veterans in Data Centers," available here (www.strategitcom.com/podcasts) or on your favorite podcast platform.

Talent Shortage Solutions

- Companies need to stop relying on computers (ATS systems) to weed out potential candidates because they don't have degrees. Companies that clearly state a degree as a requirement will not likely get non-degreed applicants. Requiring a degree knocks out roughly 63 percent of men and women who could be otherwise highly qualified and hit the ground running.
- Our veterans are highly skilled on our tax dollars and represent another source of talent for both trades and some degreed positions. Veterans cross many demographics. There is a direct correlation

between multiple jobs there and the needs of this industry. I applaud the efforts of the companies that work to put vets to work in civilian jobs.
- Relevant experience should be sought after, not discarded as "too expensive," "overqualified," or other terms that can easily equate to ageism, decreasing diversity. Credentials and experience decrease OJT training time and provide for more immediate productivity. Degrees are not necessarily an indicator of the skills required, as often the curriculum hasn't changed as fast as technology needs.
- Tech needs to embrace and provide outreach to trades, skills, and others by providing more outreach than STEM alone (although this is *critical*). Several of the data center supporting trade occupations are highly specialized. Losing talent to other verticals creates a perpetual cycle of new-hire training. Furthermore, trade talent can easily transition into meaningful operations positions. For instance, HVAC, power, and construction management are all transition-ready careers for data center operations and maintenance.
- Companies need to be more willing to embrace remote workforces where possible. Remote and hybrid work opens opportunities for additional talent resources amongst those who cannot physically move, are needed as caregivers, are raising children, etc. As long as the work gets done per the required timelines, it isn't always necessary for a person to occupy a corporate office seat daily. Video conferencing is mature.
- Equal pay is a *critical* incentive. Companies should advertise job salary ranges. Salary

advertising provides an incentive for people to seek out jobs in those occupations. Attracting new talent and diversity is a necessity.
- Certification programs and skills need to be on par with degrees where possible. HR and recruiters need a clear understanding of required and transferrable skills to evaluate resumes with vision. This is going to require time and attention of hiring managers. Just like procurement, HR may not be technical enough to select parallel skills.
- Data centers can make it a point to do business with those committed to becoming part of the solution to diversity and gender parity.

As the workforce reaches retirement age, the requisitions for skilled labor will not diminish. The need for diversity is as strong today as ever. Companies that are actively working on solutions deserve applause.

Mentors and Sponsors

I cannot stress the importance of mentors and sponsors. As mentioned before, your network is everything, and these are folks you want in your network! Mentors can be anyone. Pick someone in a job or career level you aspire to be in one day. Pick someone in the industry for the best results. They can help with career aspirations and help expand your knowledge in and around what you do. Industry professionals help navigate the ins and outs of topics you don't know. Face it; it's hard to know what you don't know. Your first mentor may not be your last or only mentor. Sometimes, mentors come and go due to fit, results, career changes, etc. Don't give up if it doesn't work out the first time.

When your mentors become sponsors, they are engaged on another level. Sponsors will bring up your name when you are not in the room and advocate for you and your career. These people will help with promotions, alternative employment, etc. Mentors can certainly become sponsors.

The mentee in the relationship needs to be ready to put in the work. Some organizations have mentee/mentor programs. Some programs have specific frameworks for their members to follow, while some leave it up to those involved to sort it out. Both are worthwhile. Just understand that it is up to the mentee to clearly communicate their goals to get help in achieving them. You cannot expect your mentor to be a mind reader. You also cannot expect to have results within a short meeting. It will take work, but it will be worth the effort.

To get a mentor, ask. It's generally quite simple. The number of people willing to help will amaze you. One can find mentors and sponsors in trade organizations, employment, churches, social circles—pretty much anywhere. Your mentor doesn't have to be like you, either. In fact, mentorship from someone quite different can add depth and dimension to your hard and soft-skill portfolios. If you're looking to move into management, the more input from diverse people, the better manager you'll become from exposure to varied viewpoints.

Sometimes, the mentee has no clear indication of their needed areas for help. A good mentor will discuss career paths and ways to help the mentee achieve success. A mentor should be someone you feel comfortable expressing your feelings and needs to. Conversely, the mentee should be willing to accept constructive criticism and guidance for the relationship to work.

At a minimum, when looking for a mentor, be able to answer these questions:

1. Where (in general) do you want to go in your career?
2. What are your immediate needs in the next 30 days?
3. How much time can you commit to success?
4. What specific needs do you have for the next 90 days?
5. Why do you feel you need a mentor?

Remember, you are asking someone for their time. Be courteous and kind with the gift you are receiving. If the mentorship isn't working for you, be prepared to do some mirror economics before finding another one. Most people will have several informal and formal mentors as they progress. Sometimes, mentoring someone else coming up will give insight into things to ask your mentor. The diversity that comes from multiple insights, both as mentor and mentee, is invaluable to career and personal growth. If you really want to get creative, volunteer for a student tech organization and just listen. Learning while giving is rewarding on all levels.

RESUME TIPS

Multiple employment surveys show that most jobs (up to 85%) are filled through networking, leaving about 15% of positions being filled online. Applicant tracking systems (ATS) collect resumes for companies. These systems work from keywords; as a submitter, you may need to revamp your resume multiple times to match those keywords.

There aren't standard definitions of jobs in this industry. Each organization may have different criteria for a job posting. READ THE POSTING thoroughly before submitting your resume. Make sure your resume bullets match the keywords in the posting. If you don't have matching skills, look for soft skills you can directly translate into that particular job. If you aren't sure which skills will translate the best, look for people with the title you aspire to and ask. Join groups on social media sites that pertain to your interests. These are great places to network.

Don't fall into some of the fodder surrounding resumes and jobs. For instance, don't change your name to initials to hide your gender. When companies want to diversify, you may get passed over in a manual resume review. Be honest.

Check your references. Believe it or not, the people you think will say good things about you may not. Tell them if there are specifics about your career or interests that you would like your references to highlight. Don't surprise a reference. Allow them to be prepared to advocate for you correctly.

Don't get caught up in buzzwords. While some professional resume writers offer great advice, some throw in a lot of industry buzzwords that don't equate to actions or accomplishments. Fluff won't get you hired. Instead, as you list your bullet points, think along the lines of items you could use to ask for a raise. The bullets should relate to actions you took that facilitated some end. Don't use the actual job description or list what are a given. Remember, the goal is to stand out. So brag (a little), even if it's hard to do. You are selling your skills and commitment to a company.

The Interview

The STAR method (Situation, Task, Action, and Results) of interviewing is the most popular used today. It is advantageous to look up some potential questions and formulate your answers.

- **S**ituation – Describe the situation clearly, be sure to state the problem and put it in context.
- **T**ask – Describe the challenges brought about by the situation.
- **A**ction – What did you do to correct the action?
- **R**esults – Shine! Let them know the excellent outcome of your actions.

You will hear questions such as, "Name a time you were in a difficult situation and explain how you resolved that situation." Look at several examples, and make sure you are comfortable with your answers.

Interview the company, too. Do your homework. Look at stock reports, interview other employees, look at interviewers' profiles, etc. Remember, this is *your* career. While it is necessary to have a job, taking a job that isn't a fit for you will only lead to frustration. Find out how the company supports employees. Ask for their mission statement. Be diligent and kind.

Always, and I mean *always*, follow up with a thank-you note. This courtesy is underrated. A thank-you note shows you appreciate the interviewer's time and the opportunity, and (the best part) is it puts you in front of the interviewer again. Highlight a couple of points to "refresh" their mind as to why you are THE BEST fit. If you are not the best fit, highlight some steps you plan to take in the first 90 days to win them over.

Look around on job sites and investigate their job descriptions. Remember, not all companies use the same definitions. Ask people in those jobs if they will give you five or ten minutes to answer some questions. Have the questions in writing so you can get the answers in the format of *their* choice. Do mock interviews. Listen to podcasts. Several on our site include people from all walks of life around the data center industry. You can gain great insight from listening to these industry experts (link in the references section). The Digital Foundation Podcast series from Infrastructure Masons is another insightful podcast.

Use cover letters. If you aren't sure what to include, you can always search, but in general:

- Introduce yourself briefly. Think of your favorite book. The intro is the hook. Don't lose them before you even start.
- List your skills and what you bring to the table. If they are parallel skills, list why they are essential to this position.
- Sell them or use a call to action. Leave the cover letter on a positive note.
- Don't use unnecessary words or punctuation!!!! (Like those exclamation points.) Be concise.
- Numbers tend to stand out. Use statements like:

- Saved the company 50% by implementing the new _____ software system.
- Increased productivity by 20% by changing territory responsibilities.
- My efforts saved customers 75% through alternative designs.

ALPHABETICAL JOB LISTINGS (SOME ANYWAY)

This list is not exhaustive by any means. Some positions apply to most companies, like human resources, benefits, accounting, travel, procurement (although technical procurement is a specialty), reception, office administrators, help desk, CRM, ERP, and other back-office positions. If you have skills that will translate into any of these positions, a foot in the door can lead to many other opportunities within the industry. Every piece you read above translates to multiple positions. We will follow the order in the book from site selection, build, to operations. Below is a listing of *some* of the jobs in the mission-critical industry.

Jobs in Site and Selection

- Accountants and CPAs
- Architects
- Brokers
- Civil drafters
- Code and AHJ personnel
- Communications providers and agents
- Community liaisons
- Company real estate resource and planning
- Consultants
- Crane operators
- Design/Build
- Engineering (civil, mechanical, electrical, industrial)
- Fuel companies, tanks, delivery, logistics
- Heavy equipment operators
- Insurance
- LEED, BREAM, green building professionals
- Legal

- Manufacturer, sales, engineering, presales, event planners, etc.
- Microgrid and renewable companies
- OSP specialists
- Power and utility companies
- Power brokers
- Procurement
- Project management
- Real estate
- Resource coordinators
- Security services
- Shipping and receiving
- Substation designers
- Sustainability practices
- Travel
- Truck drivers and equipment movers
- Zoning specialists

Build (all the above plus…)

- Carpenters
- Commissioning agents
- Construction Project Managers
- Consultants
- Customer liaisons
- DCIM and management
- Drafting and Designers
- Engineering
- Electricians, journeymen, and apprentices
- Exchange and communications personnel
- Fire system designers
- Firestop and fire detection companies
- Help desk and support personnel
- HVAC engineers, controls technicians, technicians

- Interior design
- Landscapers
- Low voltage technicians
- Manufacturers' representatives
- Masons, concrete professionals
- Modular building personnel
- NOC equipment sales, screens, etc.
- Office equipment suppliers
- Owner's representatives (interface between construction companies and owner's interests)
- Pathway and space manufacturers and installers
- Perimeter security
- Plumbers and pipe fitters
- Presales engineers (may or may not be degreed engineers)
- Project managers
- OSHA and Occupational Safety
- Quality assurance and root cause analysis teams
- Raised floor sales and installation
- Robotics programmers and testers
- Roofers
- Safety inspectors, Safety personnel
- Sales and support for all components (building materials, interiors, raised floor, cable tray, cabling, cabinets, electronics and equipment, sensors, building components, fuel and tanks, microgrids, fuel cells, etc.)
- Security and cybersecurity personnel
- Sheet metal technicians
- Standards auditors and AHJs
- Training
- Webmasters, developers
- Welders

Installation and Operations (most of the above plus...)

- AI and big data administrators
- Asset controls
- Cloud resources, architects, database administrators, cybersecurity, ERP, CRM, etc. (way too many to name them all)
- Coding careers
- Coding professions (as appropriate)
- Community liaisons
- Compliance managers
- Conservation associates, water usage effectiveness, carbon usage effectiveness, etc.
- Consumables sales (air filtration supplies, fuel and fuel conditioners, anti-static mats, fiber cleaners, labeling, termination equipment, etc.)
- Data center operations personnel and managers
- Data center technicians
- DCIM administrators
- Decommissioning agents
- Drafters
- Electrical and battery company sales, support, engineering, and maintenance
- Engineering support
- Event planners
- Facilities management, facilities operation
- HVAC companies
- Heavy equipment maintenance
- Innovation thought leaders
- Intelligent hands/remote hands
- Internal IT staff
- ITAD (IT asset destruction)
- Janitorial and cleaning services
- Low voltage technicians and RCDDs

- Maintenance and troubleshooting
- Marketing
- Moving companies (moving into a data center is specialized)
- Networking, server, storage and cloud administrators, coders, technicians, etc.
- NOC personnel, administrators, etc.
- Procurement and vendor management
- Project managers
- Quality assurance and quality control
- Raw goods and materials handling
- RCA practices
- Sales
- Sales for all internal components
- Security
- Standards auditors – operations
- Sustainability and ESG
- Telecommunications sales and support
- Training

Supporting the Industry

- Certifications and training
- Educational resource development
- EHS Auditors
- Engineering and new product development
- Green, sustainability, and ESG concerns
- Professional association personnel
- Publications and technical writing
- Sales and service
- Speakers and podcast representation
- Standards consultants and auditors
- Think tanks and research firms
- Trade shows and events

APPENDIX A – REFERENCED CODES AND STANDARDS

The below-listed standards and codes are a partial listing. Many countries and localities maintain their own codes. Therefore, individual sections of each are not referenced. Concerning standards, the primary standard is listed. It is recommended that documents reference the latest version. It is not always possible to predict the publication of new revisions without active standards participation or some source of information (manufacturer, consultant, designer). Purchasing the standards online is always an option.

As some bids will span current and newer (to be published) revisions, referencing as shown below (reference the main code—latest revision and all addendums) is a suggested practice to assure that construction and installation practices are current. In some cases, the standards bodies have collaborated on the standard's development. Include relevant trade associations as needed. Any interoperability requirements should also be listed.

Lastly, the AHJ has the final say. Touching base with an AHJ early in the specification process will assure that the facility complies with all local codes. Noncompliance is costly, disrupting, and can lead to a denial of (or loss of) the site's certificate of occupancy until the site rectifies the infractions.

Best practice guides can also be listed if they apply to the project. If manufacturer guidelines are pertinent to warranty or performance guarantees, reference them, too.

Applicable Codes in the US

While every country has their own codes, some countries follow the US. Check your own code enforcement for both national, regional, and local code adherence.

- National Electrical Code NEC (latest edition)
- National Electrical Safety Code NESC (latest edition)
- Occupational Safety and Health Act OSHA (latest edition)
- International Building Code (latest edition)
- Local/State codes

Applicable National and International Standards and Other Requirements

- ANSI/TIA – 455: Fiber Optic Test Standards (most current revision with addendums)
- ANSI/TIA – 942: Telecommunications Standard for Data Centers (most current revision with addendums)
- TIA – 526: Optical Fiber Systems Test Procedures (most current revision with addendums)
- ANSI/TIA – 568: Series of Standards (most current revisions with addendums)
- ANSI/TIA – 569: Commercial Building Standard for Telecommunication Pathways and Spaces (most current revision with addendums)
- ANSI/TIA – 606: The Administration Standard for the Telecommunications Infrastructure of Commercial Buildings (most current revision with addendums)
- ANSI/TIA – 607: Commercial Building Grounding and Bonding Requirements for Telecommunications (most current revision with addendums)
- ANSI/TIA – TSB67: Transmission Performance Specifications for Field Testing of Unshielded Twisted Pair Cabling Systems.

- ANSI/TIA – TSB75: Additional Horizontal Cabling Practices for Open Offices
- NECA/FOA 301: Standard for Installing and Testing Fiber Optic Cables (most current revision with addendums)
- NECA/BICSI 568: Standard for Installing Commercial Building Telecommunications Systems (most current revision with addendums)
- IEEE 802.3 series: Local Area Network Ethernet Standard, including the IEEE 802.3z Gigabit Ethernet Standard (most current revisions with addendums including all PoE standards)
- ISO/IEC IS 11801: Generic Cabling for Customer Premises (most current revision)
- BICSI: BICSI Telecommunications Cabling Installation Manual (most current revision)
- BICSI: BICSI Telecommunications Distribution Methods Manual TDMM (most current revision)
- Underwriters' Laboratories: UL 444 – Communications Cables (most current revision)
- Underwriters' Laboratories: UL 910 – Standard for Safety Tests for Flame-Propagation and Smoke-Density Values for Electrical and Optical-Fiber Cables Used in Spaces Transporting Environmental Air (most current revision)
- IEC/TR 61000-5-2 Ed 1.0 and amendments "Electromagnetic Compatibility EMC – Part 5: Installation and mitigation guidelines – Section 2: Earthing and Cabling (most current revision)
- ISO/IEC 11801 Ed3.0 and amendments Information Technology – Generic Cabling for Customer Premises (or most current revision)

APPENDIX A – REFERENCED CODES AND STANDARDS

- CENELEC EN 50173:2000 and amendments "Information Technology – Generic Cabling Systems"
- The facility must be fitted with a telecommunications main busbar. In the data center, if there is a raised floor, the floor must be installed with the appropriate grounding grid.
- All metal components shall be connected to the grounding/bonding system in accordance with local codes.
- All penetrations through walls and other required areas shall be fitted with appropriate fire-stopping as outlined in local codes and shall be UL Classified to ASTM E814UL1479 and approved by the local AHJ as complying with the material specified by the designated engineer of record.
- Australia/New Zealand **AS 11801.5:2019** Information technology – Generic cabling for customer premises Data centres standard.
- AS/NZS 11801.1:2019 Information technology – Generic cabling for customer premises general requirements.
- AS/NZS 3084:2017 Telecommunications installations – Telecommunications pathways and spaces for commercial buildings,
- AS/NZS 3085.1:2004 Telecommunications installations – Administration of communications cabling systems – Basic requirements.
- AS/NZS 14763.2:2020 Implementation & Operation of customer premises cabling planning & installation.
- AS/NZS 30129 Our version of TIA/EIA 607.

CPSIA information can be obtained
at www.ICGtesting.com
Printed in the USA
JSHW031037061222
34407JS00015B/23